David Scott's Guide to
Investing in Bonds

Other books on finance and investments
by David L. Scott

David Scott's Guide to Investing in Bonds

David L. Scott

Professor of Accounting and Finance

Houghton Mifflin Company
Boston • New York

This publication is designed to provide accurate and authoritative information in regard to the subject matter covered. It is sold with the understanding that neither the author nor the Publisher is engaged in rendering legal,
accounting, or other professional advice with respect to this publication. If,
as a direct result of information supplied through this publication, legal
advice or other expert assistance is required, the services of a competent
professional person should be sought.

Copyright © 2004 by David L. Scott.
All rights reserved.

Visit our website: www.houghtonmifflinbooks.com

ISBN-13: 978-0-618-35327-9
ISBN-10: 0-618-35327-5

Library of Congress Cataloging-in-Publication Data
Scott, David Logan, 1942-
  [Guide to investing in bonds]
  David Scott's Guide to investing in bonds / David L. Scott.
      p. cm.
Edition for 1997 published under title: The guide to investing in bonds.
c1997.
Includes index.
  ISBN 0-618-35327-5
  1. Bonds. I. Title: Guide to investing in bonds. II. Title.
  HG4651.S36 2004
  332.63'23--dc22

                                                        2003027520

Manufactured in the United States of America

Book design by Joyce C. Weston
Sample bond offering statement on p. 87 courtesy of Thomaston-Upson
County Office Building Authority.

QWM 10 9 8 7 6 5 4 3 2 1

Contents

Introduction

Although all bonds represent debt, not all debt is created equal. Thus, not all bonds are the same. Bonds have substantial differences including maturity length, interest payments, guarantees, tax consequences, and the risk of not being paid. Bonds have so many differences that it is not enough to decide to invest in bonds simply because ownership will increase your current investment income. When you decide to add bonds to your investment portfolio, you will be faced with a whole host of decisions such as:

- Should I buy bonds issued and guaranteed by a corporation, a municipality or state, or the U.S. Treasury?
- Should I consider buying bonds that are denominated in a foreign currency?
- Should I purchase bonds that have long maturities and relatively high yields or is it better to stick with a conservative stance and buy short-term bonds?
- Does it matter whether I buy a bond that sells at a price higher or lower than the bond's face value?
- Which measures of a bond's yield are most relevant and which should I use in making my investment decision?
- Should I consider investing in bonds that pay tax-exempt interest or is it better to choose bonds that pay taxable interest?
- Is it wise to avoid zero-coupon bonds that pay no current interest even though the overall yields are higher than bonds with coupons?
- Can I rely on a bond's quality credit rating?

- Are U.S. savings bonds competitive with other types of corporate or U.S. government bonds?
- How can I decide if the relatively high returns available on low-quality debt justify the risk of owning these securities?

Many issues are relevant to bond investments, but you probably get the point; more than a superficial knowledge of bonds is required if you expect to make investment choices that will benefit you most. You don't just buy a bond, but rather a particular bond that has specific characteristics. Bonds tend to be relatively safe investments in terms of owners receiving the promised payments, but you can suffer disappointment and financial damage if you purchase debt securities without adequate knowledge.

This *Guide to Investing in Bonds* provides the knowledge you will need to make intelligent decisions regarding bond investments. The content is designed for relatively inexperienced investors who have a desire to learn the basics of investing in bonds. Perhaps you recently reinvested money from a matured certificate of deposit (CD) in yet another CD with a disappointing yield and have decided to diversify into other investments, but you want to avoid risky alternatives. This book provides information about the various types of bonds that are available for purchase and the risks that each of these bonds entail. You will also learn the reasons that bond values fluctuate and the investment choices that can minimize the risk of these fluctuations. There is also information to help determine if you can benefit from owning municipal bonds that pay tax-exempt income.

Chapter 6 is devoted to a discussion of investing in ready-made bond portfolios including mutual funds, closed-end investment companies, and unit investment trusts. You may find that investment companies or unit investment trusts are a superior choice compared to individual bond issues. You will also find information about the differences in fees that exist among the several thousand investment companies that specialize in bond investments. Fees are especially important for bond investors who are mostly interested in current income and are willing to shop around for an extra one tenth of 1 percent in yield.

Chapter 7 discusses one of the most important topics faced by any investor: the risks that investors must face. In this chapter you will learn about the risks likely to be encountered when you choose to invest in bonds, including how you can go about reducing these risks. You don't want to invest in a bond and then be surprised by the extent of the bond's price volatility or the difficulty you encounter in selling the bond prior to maturity. You also don't want to be surprised by an early redemption when you are likely to be faced with reinvesting the principal at a reduced yield. All these risks can be determined prior to making an investment decision. It is possible to avoid most risks, but first you have to know the risks that exist.

The final chapter identifies selected sources of bond information you are likely to need. Sources are provided for current information on the condition of the credit markets. You will be able to locate information such as the number of shares of stock that can be obtained in exchange for a particular convertible bond, or whether a bond can be redeemed prior to the scheduled maturity. The Internet has become a major source of information about bond investments and is addressed in the final chapter.

Bonds provide a safety net for investors who normally invest only in stocks. Read this book and you will better understand how to construct your own safety net.

David L. Scott
Valdosta, Georgia

David Scott's Guide to Investing in Bonds

1   Fundamentals of Bonds

A bond is a security that represents a debt on the part of the bond's issuer (the borrower) and a loan on the part of the bond's owner (the lender, or creditor). Bonds are issued by businesses and by public organizations that seek investors to help pay for real estate, new and used equipment, airplanes, athletic stadiums, highways, current expenses, and a host of other needs. Most bond agreements require that the borrower pay periodic interest and, on a specified date, repay the money that was borrowed. Although all bonds exhibit certain similarities, significant differences often exist among individual bond issues including different bond issues from the same issuer.

The enormous amount of borrowing during the 1980s and 1990s by private and public organizations resulted in hundreds of billions of dollars of annual bond issues. Institutional investors such as commercial banks, mutual funds, insurance companies, and pension funds used their owners' and customers' money to purchase the biggest portion of this debt. However, individual investors attracted by the interest income acquired an increasing share of new bond issues. Corporate and government bonds have increasingly served individuals as substitutes for savings accounts, certificates of deposit, and various types of investment products sold by life insurance companies.

Why Organizations Issue Bonds

Organizations must acquire assets and pay employees in order to be able to supply the products and/or services they sell. Businesses require buildings, equipment, desks, machines, pencils, materials, and so forth. Businesses also need money to pay their employees. Governmental organizations require many of these same assets; they may also need to build parks, acquire missiles and tanks, buy garbage trucks, construct roads, and feed the homeless. All of these assets and activities require money—more money than most private and public organizations have available.

A major portion of the funds that are required by businesses and governments is supplied by normal operations. Manufacturing companies such as Ford Motor Company and Alcoa obtain most of their needed funds from the sale of products. BellSouth Corporation, a domestic communications firm, generates most of its needed funds from revenues that are earned from the sale of the firm's services. Likewise, states, cities, and counties obtain most of their required funds from tax receipts and fees.

Beyond the revenues from normal operations, businesses and governments typically must obtain additional funds from outside sources to meet their financial requirements. Just as most individuals are unable to purchase a home or automobile without financial assistance from a lender, most businesses must seek supplementary funds to pay for inventories, equipment, and buildings, and state and local governments solicit lenders that provide financing to pay for land acquisition and the construction of college buildings, bridges, and highways.

What Bonds Represent

Bonds are financial assets that evidence debt owed by organizations that borrow money. When you purchase a bond, you become a lender, or creditor, who is entitled to interest and the eventual repayment of the principal amount (also called the *face value*) represented by the bond. The loan agreement for a particular bond issue may specify that the entire principal of the loan is to be repaid in several months or it may permit the borrower to retain the funds for many years. Some agreements require that the borrower repay a portion of the principal amount each year while other agreements allow the borrower to retain the entire amount of the loan until a specified date. The term *bond* is generally reserved for a long-term debt although the media often use the word to refer to virtually all types of public and private debt.

Some of the important details about a bond, including the borrower, principal amount, interest rate, and the owner's name, are printed on the face of the certificate. Additional information on the back of the certificate might include early redemption dates and a section for endorsement by the owner in the event the bond is sold to someone else. Most investors choose to leave bonds in their brokerage account rather than take delivery and thus do not ever see a certificate. Some borrowers do not issue certificates. Complete details regarding a bond issue are included in a formal written agreement (officially called an *indenture agreement*) that is published shortly before the bonds are issued. A trustee, normally a commercial bank, is appointed and paid by the issuer to ensure that the terms of the indenture are carried out in the manner prescribed in the agreement. For example, the trustee makes certain that interest is paid in a timely manner and redemptions occur as scheduled. The trustee also verifies that any security pledged for the loan remains available for lenders to claim in the event the borrower fails to make interest payments.

Most bonds require the borrower to pay bondholders periodic interest with the dates and amounts of the payments established when the bonds are issued. Bonds typically specify that equal interest payments be made every six months until the debt is completely repaid by the borrower. In most cases the debt is repaid on a maturity date specified in the original loan agreement. Bonds are occasionally repaid prior to the specified maturity. The borrower that issued the bonds has no further obligation to its former lenders (bondholders) after the bonds have been redeemed.

Many individuals have the mistaken impression that once acquired, a bond must be held until it is redeemed at maturity. In fact, bonds are negotiable financial instruments that can be transferred from one investor to another investor in the same manner that shares of stock are transferred. Transfer of a bond is a relatively simple process that requires the current owner to endorse the back of the certificate. Although not required, nearly all investors utilize the services of brokerage firms to locate buyers and transfer the bonds to the new owner. Many investors acquire bonds with no intention to hold the bonds until the scheduled maturity date. Other investors buy bonds with the expectation of holding the securities until they mature.

No limitation is placed on the number of times a particular bond can be transferred between investors. A bond issued by the

Tip Ask your broker for an explanation of any fees you will be charged not only to buy and sell securities, but to maintain an account. Some firms charge an annual fee to maintain a brokerage account. Other firms charge a fee to deliver a bond certificate. Obtain information on a brokerage firm's fee structure prior to opening an account and placing a trade.

Tennessee Valley Authority (or any other issuer) can be purchased today and resold to another investor any time prior to the date the issuer redeems the bond. The sale can occur a week, a month, or several years after a bond is purchased. You can even resell the bond on the same day it is purchased. A bond can be resold regardless of whether it was purchased from the issuer on the original issue date or was bought after the issue date from another investor. The rights to which you are entitled as a bondholder are transferred to the new owner at the time a bond is sold. The person to whom you sell the bond can, in turn, resell the bond to yet another investor. One thing you cannot normally do is force the borrower to repurchase or redeem the bond prior to the scheduled maturity. You, or, more likely, your broker, must locate another investor who wishes to purchase the bond at a price that is agreeable to the two of you. On the other hand, the borrower is often permitted to redeem the bond on specified dates prior to the scheduled maturity. These early redemptions, termed *calls*, can be a major headache for bondholders. Early redemptions are discussed later in this chapter.

Features of Bonds

The value of a bond depends both on the bond's particulars and on certain outside factors. Important features of a bond include the dollar amount of its annual interest payments, the length of time before the principal is to be repaid, and the confidence of investors that the borrower will meet its obligations. Additional valuation factors include the level of market interest rates (for example, the interest rate banks are paying on certificates of deposit) and the condition of the credit markets. Depending upon what has occurred with respect to the issuer's financial strength and to market rates of interest since the bond was purchased, a sale is likely to result in your receiving a price different than what you paid when the bond was purchased. You are guaranteed to receive a bond's face value only when a bond is held until the scheduled maturity date. Full payment of the bond's principal assumes that the borrower remains solvent and is able to repay the loan. Some of the most important features of a bond are listed in Figure 1.

A bond's face value and market value are two different things. *Face value* is the amount the borrower will pay the bondholder on the bond's maturity date. *Market value* refers to the current value or market price of a bond. Market value is the price you would pay now to purchase the bond or the price you would receive now if you sold the bond. A bond's market price fluctuates but its face value remains constant; thus, market value and face value frequently are different. You may be able to purchase

Figure 1 ■ Important Features of a Bond

Coupon Rate	The percentage rate that, combined with the principal amount, determines the amount of the annual interest payments
Principal	The face amount of the bond that will be repaid at maturity
Maturity Date	The date the principal is scheduled for repayment
Call Provision	The right of the borrower to redeem the bond prior to maturity
Collateral	Assets that are pledged against the debt
Put Provision	The right of the bondholder to force the borrower to redeem the bond prior to the scheduled maturity
Credit Quality Rating	An independent judgment that the borrower will fulfill the bond's terms

a particular corporate bond for $900 even though the bond has a $1,000 face value. The $100 discount you receive and are certain to recover at maturity may make this bond seem like an outstanding investment opportunity, but there is certain to be a reason why the bond sells below its face value. The discount is most likely caused by the bond's annual interest payment not being competitive with the interest payments available from bonds currently being issued. For example, you wouldn't pay par value for a bond with $40 annual interest payments when new bonds of similar risk and maturity are being issued at par with $50 interest payments.

Interest Payments

The amount and dates of a bond's interest payments are established at the time a bond is issued. An issuer must set a competitive interest rate in order to attract investors who will purchase the security. Thus, the interest rate a borrower must pay to sell a bond issue depends upon the returns that investors can earn on other investments at the time the bond is issued. If market rates of interest are relatively high when a bond is issued, a new bond issue will have to specify large interest payments in order to attract buyers. A bond issued during a period of low interest rates will permit the borrower to pay a relatively small amount of interest and still find investors who wish to own the bond.

The bond's principal, or face value, in combination with the coupon rate that is established on the issue date, determine the annual dollar amount of a bond's interest payments. For example, a bond with a face value of $1,000 and a coupon rate of 7 percent will pay annual interest equal to 7 percent of $1,000, or $70. The coupon rate, principal amount, and annual interest payments remain constant throughout the life of most bonds.

Generally, a bond's coupon is established at a level that will permit the issuer to sell the bonds at or near to face value. A limited number of bond issues have very low coupon rates or even zero-coupon rates that cause the bonds to be issued at large discounts from face value. Suppose a borrower wishes to issue a bond with a 3-percent coupon and $1,000 face value at a time when the market rate of interest for similar securities is 5 percent. Lenders will be attracted to this bond only if it is issued at a substantial discount from its face value of $1,000. In this instance, the bond must be issued at a low enough price that buyers can earn the current market return of 5 percent. Bonds issued with relatively low coupons are called *original issue, deep-discount bonds* because of the low issue price compared to the face value. Bonds that are issued without any annual interest payments, that is, a coupon rate of zero, are called *zero-coupon bonds*. A borrower that issues bonds at a deep discount from face value is choosing to postpone a large portion or the entire cost of the loan until the bonds are redeemed at maturity.

Virtually all bonds pay annual interest in two installments, six months apart. An 8-percent coupon bond with a $1,000 face value will pay $80 annual interest in two $40 payments. The semiannual payment dates are determined at the date of issue and remain the same throughout the bond's life. For example, a bond agreement may specify that interest will be paid April 1 and October 1 each year until the bond is redeemed. From an investor's standpoint, semiannual payments are preferable to annual payments. An investor who buys a bond between interest payment dates must reimburse the seller for interest that has accrued since the last interest payment date. If you purchase a bond two months after the last interest payments, you are required to pay the seller two months' interest. This is only fair because your first interest payment will represent six months' interest even though you have held the bond only four months.

Maturities

A bond's *maturity* is the date the issuer is required to redeem the bond and repay the debt. *Maturity length* refers to the number of years and months until the bond is scheduled for redemption. Borrowers enter into loan agreements that last for days, weeks, months, years, and decades. Both businesses and governmental organizations arrange a large proportion of short-term borrowing with institutional lenders such as commercial banks rather than by selling securities in a public offering. Borrowers that seek short-term loans with a public sale of securities often issue the securities in such large denominations that individual investors are excluded as potential buyers. Individual investors tend to be interested in bonds with maturity lengths of several years to several decades.

Bonds issued with maturities of under 5 years are generally classified as short-term. Bonds issued with maturities of 5 to 10 years are considered to be intermediate-term debt. Long-term bonds have maturities of more than 10 years. Borrowers sometimes issue bonds that have maturities of 30 years and over. A few firms have issued bonds with maturities of 100 years. Following the date of issue a bond's maturity length becomes progressively shorter as time elapses and the bond moves toward its scheduled maturity. Long-term bonds that have been outstand-

> **Tip** Select bonds with maturities that are compatible with your investment goals. It is comforting to know that bonds will be maturing in the years when you are likely to need cash. Don't be overly influenced by the lower interest rates on bonds of shorter maturities if you are likely to require the funds sooner rather than later. Bonds sold prior to maturity may bring a price of less than par value.

ing for a number of years become intermediate-term bonds, and intermediate-term bonds finally become short-term bonds. Even though individual investors are often precluded from purchasing short-term debt securities that are part of new issues, bonds with short-term maturities can be acquired by purchasing from other investors debt securities that have been outstanding for several years.

It is important to select bonds with scheduled maturities that are appropriate for your investment requirements. Important differences exist between bonds with short maturity lengths and bonds with long maturity lengths, and bonds in each category have distinct advantages and disadvantages. Bonds with long maturity lengths are subject to greater variations in market value and generally offer higher yields compared to bonds with short maturity lengths. A proper choice of maturity depends on your investment goals and the types and amounts of investments you already own.

Early Redemptions

A bond issuer may find it advantageous to retire a portion or all of a bond issue prior to the scheduled maturity. For example, a corporation may issue bonds with a 25-year maturity and decide 10 years later that it would like to redeem the bonds 15 years prior to the scheduled maturity. One method of early retirement is to repurchase bonds from the investors who own them. That is, the company would buy the bonds on the open market at whatever price owners are willing to sell. Buying bonds in the open market is perfectly legitimate and bondholders should have no complaint because they can choose whether or not to sell their bonds back to the issuer.

Many indenture agreements include a provision that permits the borrower to force its bondholders to surrender their bonds many years prior to the scheduled maturity. For example, the terms of a loan agreement with a 20-year maturity may allow the borrower to redeem its bonds 10 years following the issue date. Thus, bonds issued in 2005 with a scheduled maturity of 2025 could be redeemed in 2015. Bondholders have no choice but to sell the bonds back to the issuer if the loan agreement includes a provision for an early redemption. Most long-term corporate bonds and municipal bonds allow for early redemption by issuers. Most bonds issued by the U.S. Treasury do not allow for an early redemption.

The early redemption of a bond is known as a *call*, and the price at which the bond can be redeemed, or called, is the *call price*. The terminology stems from the borrower being permitted to call its bonds away from bondholders. Dates and prices at which an issuer can call bonds are specified in the indenture agreement. The possibility of an early redemption should be a very important consideration when deciding whether to purchase a particular bond. Early redemptions mean that the principal of the loan is repaid sooner than generally expected.

Early redemptions nearly always occur to the disadvantage of bondholders even though borrowers must often pay slightly more than face value for redeemed bonds. For example, an issuer may be required to pay bondholders $1,020 for each $1,000 of principal amount for a bond issue that is called prior to maturity. Loan agreements that permit issuers to call bonds nearly always specify a period of time, generally 5 to 10 years, following the date of issue during which bondholders are protected from an early redemption. Once this period of protection has elapsed, the option of whether to call the bond is in the hands of the issuer.

If allowed, a borrower will normally redeem its bonds prior to maturity only when market interest rates have declined below the coupon rate offered on the bond. The more that market interest rates decline below a bond's coupon rate, the more

> **Tip** Call provisions are a very important consideration in selecting bonds to purchase. A call provision may result in your being required to sell the bond back to the issuer many years before the scheduled maturity date. A call will nearly always occur when market interest rates have declined and you can only reinvest your funds at a lower return.

likely the bond will be redeemed early by the issuer. If you are a borrower, why continue to pay 8 percent on an existing loan when new funds are available for only 6 percent? Suppose that 10 years ago a company issued bonds with a 25-year maturity and a coupon rate of 7 percent. If market interest rates have since declined to 5 percent, the borrower can substantially reduce its interest expense by replacing the old 7-percent debt with a new issue of 5-percent bonds. This is no different from refinancing the loan on your home when mortgage rates fall below the rate you are being charged on your existing loan.

A small number of bond issues permit bondholders to force an issuer to redeem its bonds prior to the bonds' scheduled maturity. This provision, called a *put option*, is valuable to a bondholder when interest rates have risen following issue of the bond. The put allows the bondholder to force an early redemption so the principal that is returned to the lender can be reinvested at a rate higher than is being paid by the redeemed bond. Bonds that give bondholders the right to force an early redemption are called *put bonds*.

Credit Quality

The credit quality of a bond refers to the likelihood that scheduled interest and principal will be paid in a timely manner. The credit quality of publicly traded bonds ranges from U.S. Treasury securities, long considered the standard of safety against which all other investments are measured, to high-risk bonds that may not realize their next scheduled interest payment. Not surprisingly, investors prefer bonds with a high credit quality and are willing to accept a reduced rate of return in order to own these bonds. The desire by investors for credit quality results in an inverse relationship between credit quality and yield. That is, the higher the credit quality of a bond, the lower the expected yield.

A bond's credit quality is influenced by many factors, including the financial structure (capitalization) and the revenue and cost streams of the organization that issues the bond. The bonds of a company with little debt that is a leader in a growing industry are likely to be considered as having high credit quality. Likewise, a city with a strong tax base and a moderate amount of outstanding debt will be able to issue bonds of high credit quality. At the opposite end of the credit quality spectrum, a small firm heavily in debt and an also-ran in an emerging industry will have bonds with low credit quality and a relatively high yield.

At any one time a particular borrower may have several different issues of outstanding bonds. Figure 2 (p. 14) illustrates the many different outstanding issues of long-term debt of Cincinnati-based consumer products giant, Procter & Gamble. Because different bond issues by the same borrower often have different promises, maturities, and so forth, the credit quality of a particular bond issue can be more important than the credit quality of the issuer. For example, a company may have one bond issue with a very strong promise of repayment because bondholders have a priority claim over all the firm's other lenders. Other debt issues from the same firm have an inferior claim and a reduced credit quality. Many bond indentures include specific language stating the bonds have a claim that is subordinated to other debt of the firm. Thus, two bond issues

Figure 2 ■ Long-Term Debt of the Procter & Gamble Company (June 30, 2002–in millions)

6.00% note due March 2003	$ 500
5.25% note due September 2003	750
8.00% note due November 2003	200
6.60% note due December 2004	1,000
8.33% ESOP debentures due 2003–04	212
4.00% note due April 2005	400
5.75% Euro note due September 2005	1,478
1.50% Japanese yen note due December 2005	459
4.75% note due June 2007	1,000
6.13% note due May 2008	500
6.88% note due September 2009	1,000
2.00% Japanese yen note due 2010	417
9.36% ESOP debentures due 2007–21	1,000
8.00% note due September 2024	200
6.45% note due January 2026	300
6.25% Great Britain pound note due January 2030	763
All other long-term debt	1,640
Total	**$11,819**
less current portion of long-term debt	618
Total Long-Term Debt Outstanding	**11,201**

can have substantially different credit quality despite the fact that both issues are guaranteed by the same company. The financial strength of an issuer is obviously important, but an investor who is considering the purchase of bonds must investigate the credit quality of a particular bond issue as well as the credit quality of the issuer. Bonds of different credit quality from the same issuer are a more relevant concern for investors who are interested in purchasing corporate bonds and municipal bonds than for investors planning to buy U.S. government bonds.

Judging a bond's credit quality is a complex task that involves an examination of the borrower's financial condition along with a judgment of management quality, a forecast of future revenues, and insight on likely sources of financing. The majority of investors have neither the time nor the expertise to make these judgments and are forced to rely on the analysis and ratings that are made available by bond rating agencies including Fitch, Moody's, and Standard & Poor's Corporation. Ratings grades differ slightly among the several rating firms, although AAA is the highest credit rating awarded by each firm. An AAA rating enables an issuer to borrow money at a relatively low rate of interest. Issuers do not always seek a rating for their bonds, so some bonds are issued without a credit rating. Chapter 7 includes a discussion of bond credit ratings along with a chart containing a short description of each rating category.

Why Invest in Bonds?

Most individual and institutional investors purchase bonds because of the interest income. Annual interest payments on most bonds remain unchanged, so an investor can count on receiving a steady income for a known number of years. The guaranteed stream of interest payments plus a specified date for the return of principal can produce an attractive investment for individuals seeking current investment income with the knowledge of when their investment will be returned.

Some investors purchase bonds because they anticipate an increase in the market value of the bonds. These investors expect to earn income both from interest payments and from a gain in the value of their investment. The market value of a bond will increase if the market rate of interest declines after the bond is purchased. A loan with a stated interest rate of 8 percent is a valuable asset to own when new loans are being made at a 6-percent rate of interest. Likewise, a bond with an 8-percent coupon rate will be worth more than its face value if market rates of interest decline and new bonds are being issued with coupon rates of less than 8 percent. An investor who is able to accurately forecast interest rates and purchase bonds when interest rates are relatively high will be able to earn generous interest income at the same time that the bond will increase in value. The increase in value assumes that market interest rates subsequently decline.

Although the market value of bonds is constantly changing, these changes typically are relatively small compared to changes in the market values of common stocks. Thus, investors who seek investment assets with the potential for large gains in value generally look to investments other than bonds. The important relationship between the market value of a bond and market rates of interest is very important and will be addressed throughout this book.

The Downside of Bond Ownership

Any investment has both good and bad features, and bonds are

no exception to this rule. Bond ownership can be a risky investment with possible drawbacks. One such drawback is the
potential for inflation that causes annual fixed interest payments
and the principal that will eventually be returned to deteriorate
in purchasing power. The deterioration is greater the longer the
bond is to be held. The higher the level of inflation, the more
rapid the deterioration in the purchasing power of fixed payments. Inflation may turn out to be far more serious than
expected and, in the worst case, actually exceed the return provided by a bond. Such an outcome is a bondholder's worst
nightmare.

The possibility exists, especially for owners of corporate
debt, that bondholders will not receive all of the payments that
have been promised. Although the financial claims of lenders
have priority over the claims of a company's owners, the financial condition of a business can deteriorate rapidly, especially if
a firm's managers have chosen to hide problems from the public, so that bondholders end up losing a substantial portion of
their investment. Likewise, government projects that are
financed with borrowed money may prove to be white ele-
phants that result in major losses for lenders. Manufacturing
companies, retailers, financial institutions, and cities can all go
bankrupt and leave bondholders with worthless pieces of paper.

An earlier section of this chapter pointed out that bond values vary inversely with market interest rates. If interest rates rise
after you purchase a bond the market value of your investment
will decline. In other words, the bond will be worth less than
you paid. The potential for fluctuations in value may not be a
concern unless there is a possibility you will need to sell the
bond prior to maturity. Selling a bond following a major
increase in market rates of interest means you are likely to
receive less than you paid. You can invest in high-quality bonds

and still lose a portion of your investment.

How Bonds Compare to Stocks

Although bonds and stocks are both negotiable financial instruments, few similarities exist between the two securities. Shares of stock represent ownership in a business while bonds represent a loan to a business or government entity. As part owner of a business, shares of common stock generally give you a voice in the company's management and a claim to a portion of the firm's profits. Stockholders of a corporation can earn very large profits when things go right and can suffer very large losses (although never more than 100 percent of the money invested) when things turn sour. Just ask stockholders of Enron, World-Com, and UAL, parent of United Airlines. The risks and rewards for business owners are substantial.

The stockholders of a successful business can expect the value of their ownership shares to appreciate at the same time that increased cash distributions are received from profits. A business experiencing growing sales and profits that currently pays a dividend of 35¢ per share may pay a dividend of 40¢ next year and $1.00 per share in 9 or 10 years. At the other end of the scale, a business may suffer several years of poor operating

| Tip | Bonds tend to offer greater safety than shares of preferred stock issued by the same firm. Bond owners are creditors of the issuer and have the right to be paid before owners, including owners who hold shares of preferred stock. The board of directors must vote on dividends to be paid to preferred stockholders, while interest to bondholders is a legal obligation of the borrower. |

> **Tip** Bonds should be one part of a diversified portfolio along with stocks, tangible assets including real estate, and liquid investments such as a money market account. It is risky to have all of your assets in bonds or any other single type of investment.

results and reduce or eliminate the dividends it pays to its stockholders. The poor financial performance accompanied by a reduction in dividends is likely to cause a decline in the market price of the stock. Compared to investors who own common stocks, owners of bonds do not generally experience either variations in annual income or substantial changes in the market value of their securities.

In the event that a business develops serious financial difficulties, the firm's lenders have a claim to payment for the full amount of a loan, and the claim has priority to any recovery by the firm's owners. The senior claim of bondholders is yet another reason why bonds are considered to be less risky than shares of stock issued by the same company.

Another important difference between bonds and stocks is that stocks have no scheduled date when principal is to be repaid to stockholders. In other words, shares of common stock have no maturity date. The lack of a maturity date is important because stockholders can only liquidate their investment by locating another investor who will purchase their shares. A bondholder has the option of holding the security until the scheduled maturity, at which time the bond's face amount will be paid to the bondholder.

The bottom line for investors is that a bond is a more conservative investment than common stock of the same company. The annual income from a bond's interest payments is more certain and the market value of the bond is more stable. At the same time, a bond offers less profit potential than shares of common stock. Owning common stock can make you rich (or poor) while owning bonds is only likely to keep you rich (assuming you already are).

Should You Invest in Bonds?

Bonds are an appealing investment choice when your primary investment goal is current income. Bonds are good substitutes for other income-producing investments such as long-term certificates of deposit, investment contracts offered by life insurance companies, preferred stocks, and common stocks that pay high dividends (and offer little growth in market value). Bonds are a more questionable investment choice if you are not in need of additional current income—that is, your existing income (both investment income and earned income) is adequate to meet your current and anticipated spending requirements. With substantial amounts of current income you are probably better advised to concentrate on investments that have a greater potential for gains in value.

It is generally wise to seek a balance between low-risk, income-producing investments and high-risk investments that offer appreciation potential. Investing in corporate or govern-

> **Tip** Keep accurate records for bonds (or any other investment) you acquire because the date of purchase and the price paid are required to calculate the capital gain or loss that must be reported on your tax return. You are required to report the proceeds from any bond that is sold or redeemed even if no gain or loss results.

> **Tip**
>
> Keep in mind that buying bonds denominated in a foreign currency will produce a return influenced by foreign exchange rates as well as interest rates. Your return will benefit from a strengthening of the foreign currency in which your bond is denominated and your return will suffer if the foreign currency weakens relative to the dollar.

ment bonds offsets a portion of the risks that are inherent in the ownership of other investments, particularly common stocks. The proper balance between stocks and bonds is a judgment call that depends upon several factors including your age, income, employment prospects, family status, and so forth. In general, the closer you are to retirement, the greater the proportion of your investment portfolio that should be in bonds as opposed to stocks.

Your tax situation will play a major part in the decision to invest in bonds and your choice of what types of bonds to buy. The interest income from bond ownership is less beneficial if you pay a high tax rate on current income. If a large proportion of your current income must be surrendered to federal and state tax payments, an investment that mostly offers additional current income may not be particularly desirable. On the other hand, certain types of bonds offer the potential for significant tax savings. In general, bonds issued by state and local governments pay interest that is not subject to federal taxation, whereas bonds issued by the U.S. Treasury pay interest that is not subject to state and local taxation, but is subject to federal taxation.

2   Corporate Bonds

Corporations issue a wide variety of bonds that are available for purchase by individual investors. The investment quality of corporate bonds ranges from very high-grade bonds that are considered to be nearly as safe as U.S. Treasury securities to bonds with such a questionable future that they are classified as junk. The different characteristics of various corporate bonds are an important consideration in selecting these debt securities. Corporate bonds normally provide higher pretax yields than either U.S. government bonds or municipal bonds.

A corporate bond is a corporate bond is a corporate bond. Well, sort of. Similarities certainly exist among corporate bonds so as to cause these securities to be lumped into a distinct investment category. Bonds represent debt, of course, but other important likenesses identify these securities. For example, corporate bonds are nearly always issued in $1,000 denominations and require the issuer to make fixed semiannual interest payments until a specified maturity date at which time the face value is paid to the bondholders. Interest income received from corporate bonds is taxed to bondholders at both the federal level and the state level. Interest expense is allowed as a deductible expense by the borrower in calculating corporate income taxes.

Understanding the similarities of corporate bonds is important, but understanding the differences is equally important. Corporate bonds have different maturity dates, different interest payments, different payment dates, and different provisions regarding early redemption. Corporate bonds also have different guarantees regarding the payments that are promised. For example, different companies have widely varying abilities to meet their financial obligations. In addition, many debt securities provide investors with liens on specific assets such as equipment and real estate. Other corporate bonds are secured by the added guarantee from another organization such as a bank or insurance company. The bottom line for the individual investor is that corporate bonds are different enough that you must be very selective in choosing among these securities.

How Businesses Are Financed

A business is initially formed with ownership capital called *equity* that is supplied by one or more investors who expect to participate in the firm's future profits. Suppose you and some acquaintances decide to pool your personal funds and establish a small chain of Romanian restaurants. If the members of your investment group are sufficiently wealthy and willing to risk a large amount of personal wealth on a potentially risky investment, no other financing may be required to get the project off the ground. If, however, your investment group is unable or unwilling to contribute all of the funds that are required to pay for the construction and initial operation of the planned restaurants, it will be necessary to obtain outside financing.

One possible solution is to identify and bring in additional investors who wish to become owners and would expect to receive a proportional share of the firm's anticipated profits. In addition, these new owners may demand a voice in the firm's decision making. The members of your investment group may decide they are unwilling to share control and profits with other investors, however. In any case, you may have difficulty locating other investors who will contribute ownership capital to your risky project.

Why Businesses Finance with Debt

Borrowing may present a way out of your financing dilemma. Obtaining a loan will allow your ownership group to maintain total control of the business's operations and profits because lenders do not normally participate in either management decisions or profit distributions. Borrowing will require that your business pay the lenders interest during the period the loan is outstanding. In addition, the principal amount of the loan must eventually be paid. The lender may also establish certain requirements of your firm as a condition for making a loan. For example, the loan agreement may specify that your firm maintain cash at some minimum level.

Fixed payments required by a loan agreement will cause your new company to confront financial risk that can be avoided if you rely only on equity financing from owners. If business at your restaurants turns out to be less robust than anticipated, the firm might encounter difficulty meeting the interest and principal payments stipulated by the loan agreement. An inability to make the legally required payments will have serious negative consequences for the firm and its owners.

Although borrowing places your business in a more risky financial position, you and the other owners may benefit from earning a higher return on your investment. The higher return results from having locked in a portion of the firm's financing costs (interest to the lenders) without being required to share profits among additional owners. In other words, all the firm's profits belong to the original pool of owners.

There is a limit to the amount of money that a business may reasonably borrow. Some businesses find it impossible to locate willing lenders, especially when owners have little of their own funds to invest. Individual investors and financial institutions are willing to become lenders only when they are reasonably certain that interest and principal on a loan will be paid. Many budding entrepreneurs are overly optimistic regarding the economic viability of their businesses. Outside investors who have no personal attachment to the business and who are asked to put their money at risk are likely to view the business in a more detached manner. As a result, individuals who have what they consider to be a good idea for a business may encounter difficulty locating other investors who are willing to supply capital in return for becoming either owners or lenders.

The Need for Balance Between Debt and Equity

The managers of a business generally try to strike a balance between the capital that is supplied by owners and the capital that is supplied by lenders. Figure 3 illustrates the financing methods utilized by a variety of public corporations. Notice that some firms rely heavily on borrowing to finance their assets. Other firms choose to finance almost entirely with ownership money. If a business relies too heavily on ownership capital,

Figure 3 ■ Financing Methods Used by Selected Businesses (Late 2001—in millions of dollars)

Company	Short-Term Liabilities	Long-Term Liabilities	Owner Investment
Brinker International	302	504	977
Coca-Cola	8,863	5,073	11,351
Delta Airlines	6,703	8,347	3,769
Gencorp	465	689	310
General Electric	198,904	241,295	54,824
IBM	35,119	25,580	23,614
Loral Corporation	581	2,457	1,351
PPG Industries	1,955	3,417	3,080
RJ Reynolds Tobacco	2,792	4,232	8,026
Roadway Corp.	413	307	360
Skyline Corp.	36	4	198
Union Pacific Corp.	2,692	19,284	9,575
Winn-Dixie Stores	1,110	565	812

owners' returns on their investment are penalized because profits have to be spread over many shares of ownership. On the other hand, if a business relies too heavily on debt financing, owners and lenders are both subject to an increased risk of losing their investment. Existing businesses that are heavily in debt sometimes have difficulty locating additional lenders because of concern about the ability of the business to service its debts.

Substantial amounts of publicly traded corporate debt in the United States are issued by utilities that require immense sums of money to pay for expensive power plants (some of which cost billions of dollars) and transmission facilities. Industrial corporations that engage in activities such as manufacturing and natural resource development are also major bond issuers. Telecommunications companies borrowed huge amounts of money before the industry went in the tank and its financing sources shut down in early 2001. Other categories of corporate bonds include those issued by transportation companies such as airlines and railroads and by financial companies including banks and insurers.

Fundamentals of Corporate Bonds

A corporate bond is evidence of business debt. Several types of corporate bonds are issued and will be discussed in this chapter. Nearly all publicly traded corporate debt is issued and traded in $1,000 denominations. Thus, you can purchase $1,000, $5,000, $7,000, or more of a particular corporate bond so long as your purchase is in multiples of $1,000. The minimum purchase is $1,000, which represents one bond. You will receive only one certificate for a single transaction no matter how many bonds are purchased. For example, a single certificate will be issued when you purchase $30,000 par value of a bond. Purchase another $15,000 of the same bond on a later date and you will receive a second certificate. Holding a certificate for $30,000 of a particular bond does not mean you must sell the entire $30,000 at one time. Rather, you can sell any amount of the $30,000 so long as the sale is in multiples of $1,000. Selling less than $30,000 means you must surrender the certificate and receive a new certificate for the principal amount that you continue to own.

The particulars of a corporate bond issue are spelled out in the indenture agreement that is drawn up before the bonds are initially brought to market. The indenture is a long and legalistic document that details the amount being borrowed, the size and dates of interest payments, the maturity date, early redemption provisions, collateral, the trustee charged with making certain the borrower follows through on its promises, and so forth.

Corporate bonds are initially issued at or near face value. Borrowers are able to issue bonds at face value by establishing an interest rate at the level demanded by the market at the time of issue. For example, if the current interest rate on 15-year medium-grade bonds is 6 percent, a borrowing firm is likely to establish an interest rate on a new issue of bonds at 6 percent (i.e., agree to pay annual interest of $60 for each $1,000 bond) in order to be able to sell the bonds at face value. Establishing a lower interest rate than 6 percent would force the borrower to issue the bonds at less than $1,000 in order to provide the 6-percent return investors demand.

Once a bond has been issued, its price when traded among investors in the secondary market will fluctuate with changes in market rates of interest and changes in the perception of the issuer's ability to service the debt. Thus, while you might expect to buy a newly issued bond in the primary market at face value, previously issued bonds trading among investors in the secondary market generally trade at prices above or below their $1,000 face value. Even though you may pay more or less than face value when a particular bond is purchased, it is almost a certainty that you will receive face value if the bond is held to its scheduled maturity. Purchase $5,000 principal amount of bonds at a price of $1,030 per bond and you will be charged a total of 5 times $1,030, or $5,150, even though you can expect to receive only $5,000 at maturity. Likewise, if you buy a bond for its face value on the issue date, you are unlikely to receive exactly the amount you paid if it is necessary to sell the bond prior to the scheduled maturity. The bottom line is that corporate bond investments can produce gains and losses in market value unless the bonds are purchased at face value and held to maturity.

Corporate bonds generally provide higher returns than are available either on U.S. Treasury securities or municipal bonds. Corporate bonds offer higher returns because of a greater likelihood that the terms of corporate bonds will not be met by the issuers. In general, the U.S. Treasury and most municipal borrowers are considered more creditworthy than the majority of corporations. In addition, U.S. Treasury and municipal bond issues have important tax advantages compared to corporate bonds. Interest from corporate bonds is fully taxable, whereas interest from U.S. Treasury securities escapes taxation by states and municipalities, and most municipal bond interest escapes taxation by the federal government and, occasionally, by state and local governments as well.

Interest Payments on Corporate Bonds

Most corporate bonds make semiannual interest payments that remain unchanged from the date of issue until the bonds are redeemed by the issuer. If General Electric issues $1,000 principal amount, 6-percent coupon bonds that pay $60 annual interest, an investor who buys these bonds will receive $30 per bond every 6 months until the bonds are sold or redeemed. The size of a corporate bond's fixed interest payment is the most important factor influencing the market value of the bond. Bonds with higher interest payments tend to have higher market values.

Although somewhat unusual, corporations sometimes issue floating rate notes and bonds on which the interest payments are periodically altered according to some predetermined formula. The interest adjustments to floating rate notes and bonds cause these securities to sell at a price close to par value. The interest rate on a high-quality floating rate corporate bond is related to and slightly above the interest rate on newly issued, short-term U.S. Treasury debt. Invest in a floating rate bond or note and you will encounter uncertainty regarding the amount of interest income to be earned in future years. On the positive side, floating rate bonds exhibit substantial price stability that generally permits you to sell the bonds prior to maturity at a price close to par value.

The Safety of Corporate Bonds

Credit quality is a function of a company's ability to meet a bond's scheduled interest and principal payments in a timely manner. It is also influenced by the value of any assets that secure the debt. Bonds issued by a conservatively financed company that is a leader in a growing industry will generally be of high credit quality. At the opposite end of the credit quality spectrum, a small firm that is heavily in debt and a second-tier company in an emerging industry will have difficulty borrowing money at any interest rate. Judging a corporate bond's credit quality is a complicated task that involves an examination of a

> **Tip** The credit quality of corporate bonds can change in the years following their issue. A corporation that is considered financially strong at the time a bond is issued may encounter unexpected operating difficulties and become financially weak. A decline in an issuer's credit quality is likely to cause a decline in its credit rating.

firm's current financial status, competition, and management quality along with a forecast of future operations. Most investors rely on credit rating firms to judge the credit risk of owning particular issues of corporate bonds. An expanded discussion of this important topic is in Chapter 7.

The credit quality of corporate bonds covers a wide spectrum. Corporate bonds are more risky to own than U.S. Treasury securities and, as a group, are more risky to own than municipal bonds. Corporations often rely on unpredictable revenue streams to service their debt, whereas state and local governments have the power to levy taxes. Despite the generally greater risk of corporate bonds compared to U.S. Treasury and municipal bonds, many financially strong corporations issue bonds that are considered to be of very high credit quality.

An important determinant of a corporate bond's credit quality is whether specific assets have been pledged to secure the

> **Tip** The quality of corporate debt is strongly influenced by whatever collateral, if any, is pledged by the borrower. Pledging valuable collateral that can be easily liquidated will result in a relatively high quality bond even if the issuing company has a questionable credit rating.

bond and its promised payments. Some corporate bond indentures pledge specific assets owned by the borrower as collateral for the loans. In the event the borrower defaults on the terms of the loan, bondholders can order the assets sold to satisfy their claim. Having specific assets pledged as collateral for a loan means that the bondholders are less likely to compete with other lenders in determining who gets paid in the event the borrower is unable to meet its financial obligations. The more valuable the assets that are pledged as collateral on a loan compared to the amount of money that is borrowed, the more confidence bondholders should have that they will receive the promised payments. Bonds backed by a legal claim on specific property are often called *senior bonds*, in contrast to *junior bonds* that have a secondary claim to payment.

Corporations often issue bonds that are not secured by specific assets. Interest and principal payments on these debt securities remain as legal obligations of the issuing corporation, but without particular assets identified to secure the obligations, unsecured debt is more risky to own than bonds backed by specific assets. The increased risk of owning unsecured debt means that a corporate borrower will have to offer a high interest rate in order to attract willing lenders. A large amount of outstanding corporate debt is of the unsecured variety.

Risk-averse investors prefer high-quality corporate bonds despite the lower expected return compared to more risky corporate debt. The direct relationship between the return available on a corporate bond and the bond's perceived risk is important to remember as you consider investing in debt securities. There is always a reason a corporate bond offers an especially high return in order to attract investors. After all, it is not in the interest of a business to pay more interest than necessary. Payment of an unusually high rate of interest nearly always relates to the high risk associated with owning the bond.

Maturity Lengths of Corporate Bonds

At any particular time an investor will have a wide array of bond maturity lengths from which to choose. New corporate bond issues with a variety of maturities are ordinarily brought to market each week. Some of these issues have short maturity lengths of 1 to 5 years while other issues will have maturities of 25 and 30 years. As discussed in Chapter 1, indenture agreements for long-term bonds generally contain call provisions that permit the borrower to redeem bonds prior to the scheduled maturity date. A corporate bond with an original maturity length of 25 years may end up being redeemed by the issuer only 10 years following the issue date if an early redemption is permitted by the indenture agreement and the redemption is in the interest of the borrower. It is important to remember that you cannot always count on a corporate bond to remain outstanding until the scheduled maturity. Corporate notes with short or intermediate maturities are usually not callable by the issuer.

Corporate bond indentures frequently include a sinking fund provision that requires the issuer to annually set aside a certain sum of money to retire a portion of the issue. The sinking fund requirement may be stated in terms of the initial issue or in terms of the issue that remains outstanding. It may be expressed either as a percentage or as an annual dollar amount. For example, an issuer of 20-year bonds may be required to annually retire 5 percent of the issue's initial principal beginning 10 years following the date of issue. Bonds that are retired to meet a sinking fund requirement may be purchased by the issuer in the open market or may be called from bondholders. Companies that redeem bonds to meet sinking fund requirements normally are required to pay only face value for the securities. A sinking fund requirement is sometimes advantageous to bondholders because purchases by the issuer increase trading activity and enhance the bond's liquidity (that is, make the bond easier to sell). Unfortunately, a sinking fund also creates uncertainty on the part of the investor regarding when a bond will be retired and the investor's funds returned.

Types of Corporate Bonds

Corporations issue a wide variety of bonds. Some of the differences in bond issues result from peculiar characteristics of the issuers. For example, utilities by the nature of their business tend to own substantial amounts of real property and issue a large number of bonds that are secured by real estate and buildings. Airlines issue specialized debt secured by their main assets, airplanes. Other differences among corporate bonds result from the diverse methods used by issuers to package bond issues. Borrowers and the financial advisers who assist them generally attempt to put together a bond issue so as to keep the interest cost as low as possible.

Categories of Corporate Bonds

1. *Convertible bonds*—debt securities that permit the bondholder to exchange the bonds for another asset, generally shares of the issuer's common stock. These securities are discussed more fully in the next section of this chapter.

2. *Debentures*—Long-term corporate debt that is secured by the issuer's promise of repayment but not by specific assets. The owner of a debenture is a general creditor of the issuer. All of the assets not pledged against other debt serve as collateral for a debenture and other unsecured debt. Debentures are generally issued either by businesses that have already pledged all of their assets in other loan agreements or by businesses that have such a high credit rating that they have no need to pledge assets.

3. *Guaranteed bonds*—Debt securities backed by an organization other than the issuer. For example, a large corporation may guarantee the bonds of one of its subsidiaries in order that the subsidiary can borrow at a lower rate of interest.

4. *Income bonds*—Debt securities on which the issuer is required to pay interest to lenders only if sufficient income is available. Income bonds are unusual and nearly always issued by failed companies in the process of being reorganized. Ownership of these securities entails substantial risk on the part of the investor.

5. *Junk bonds*—Debt securities of poor credit quality (and an accompanying low credit rating). Also called *high-yield bonds*, these securities are considered very risky because the borrowers may be unable to meet the terms of the bonds. Junk bonds typically offer relatively high interest rates to attract investors who accept a high risk of nonpayment. Individual investors should generally avoid the purchase of these high-risk securities, especially if insufficient funds are available to diversify among many different issues.

6. *Mortgage bonds*—Securities that grant bondholders a first mortgage on a particular property or on all of the borrower's property. Mortgage bonds are generally considered to be among the safest bonds to own because of the quality of the collateral.

7. *Subordinated debentures*—Unsecured debt securities with a claim to payments that is subordinated to virtually all the borrower's other debt including any outstanding debentures. Subordinated debentures generally subject an investor to substantial risk of not being paid and, as a result, offer unusually high yields to attract buyers.

8. *Zero-coupon bonds*—Debt securities that do not pay semian-

> **Tip**
>
> Zero-coupon corporate bonds create a tax problem for most investors who will be required to pay annual taxes on income that is received only on paper. These bonds accrue interest but do not actually pay interest. Still, owners of zero-coupon bonds must declare and pay taxes on the accrued interest that issuers annually report to the Internal Revenue Service.

nual interest and are issued at a large discount from face value. These bonds pay the face value to owners at the scheduled maturity or proportionately less than face value if the bonds are redeemed prior to maturity. An investor is taxed on the annual imputed interest income of a zero-coupon corporate bond even though no interest is actually paid by the issuer or received by bondholders until the bond is redeemed.

Convertible Bonds

Corporations sometimes issue debt securities that buyers can later exchange for shares of the issuer's common stock. Investors who purchase these securities can choose to become owners rather than creditors. Convertible securities are interesting investments and so different from regular bonds that they deserve a detailed explanation.

A convertible bond permits the bondholder to exchange the bond for a predetermined number of shares of the issuer's common stock. The bondholder, not the issuer, controls the decision of when and whether to exchange convertible bonds for shares of stock. The exchange is undertaken with the bond's issuer who will be required to issue additional shares of stock to replace the debt. Suppose a $1,000 principal amount bond issued by Wilkinson Corporation matures in 20 years and has a

6-percent coupon. The Wilkinson bond pays $60 in annual interest (6 percent of $1,000) and will be redeemed at face value by the firm on the specified maturity date. The Wilkinson bonds are identical to other corporate bonds with respect to interest and principal repayment requirements. Assume, however, that the Wilkinson issue permits bondholders to convert each bond into 50 shares of Wilkinson common stock. The

Figure 4 ■ Conversion Features of Selected Convertible Bonds

Issuer	Bond Coupon	Shares per Bond	Maturity	S&P Rating	Issue Amount (Millions)
Amazon.com	6.875 %	11.7810	02/16/10	CCC+	$ 681
Anadarko Petroleum	0.000	11.6288	03/07/20	BBB+	690
Cendant	3.875	41.5800	11/27/11	BBB	1,200
Charter Communications	4.750	38.0952	06/01/06	B-	633
GenCorp	5.750	54.2888	04/15/07	B+	150
Inco	7.750	26.1140	03/07/20	BBB-	173
Lattice Semiconductor	4.750	48.2620	11/01/06	B-	260
Mirant	5.750	131.9890	07/15/07	BB	370
Ohio Casualty	5.000	44.2112	03/19/22	BB	201
Rite Aid	4.750	153.8460	12/01/06	B-	150
Silicon Graphics	6.250	25.5363	02/01/11	CC	82
Verizon Communications	0.000	7.9380	05/15/21	A+	5,442

conversion is accomplished when bondholders return bonds to the issuer with instructions to exchange the bonds for shares of stock. If you send the issuer a $1,000 principal amount certificate and request conversion, you will receive 50 shares of stock in return. Submit a $5,000 certificate and you will receive up to 250 shares of Wilkinson stock depending upon what proportion of the bond you wish to convert. Figure 4 (p.37) illustrates the conversion feature for several convertible bond issues.

When a convertible bond is submitted for conversion (or, if bonds are being maintained in a brokerage account, your broker submits bonds for conversion), all rights are surrendered to further interest payments and repayment of principal. In place of interest and principal you will begin receiving dividends from the shares of common stock, assuming the firm's directors declare dividends. Conversion into shares of stock is at your option and the exchange cannot be reversed once the transaction is complete. After exchanging convertible bonds for shares of stock you become an owner rather than a creditor. Now your only choice is to either sell or continue to hold the stock.

Convertible bonds convey all the rights of a regular bond and have the added advantage of allowing a bondholder to switch from being a creditor to being an owner. The prerogative of a bondholder to be able to switch securities and become a stockholder is potentially very valuable because the business may prove very successful, thereby causing the firm's common stock to appreciate in value. A regular bond will fluctuate in value during the period it is outstanding, but the bond will eventually trend toward the face value as the bond approaches maturity. Common stock has considerably more upside potential than bonds and does not have to be surrendered to the issuer. Convertibles can be exchanged for a specific number of shares of stock no matter how high the value of each of these shares

> **Tip** Convertible corporate bonds offer greater potential for price appreciation than bonds that are not convertible. The market value of a convertible bond will tend to follow the market value of the stock into which the bond can be converted. On the negative side, a convertible bond's market value will be negatively affected by a decline in the market price of the stock.

climbs. In the Wilkinson example described above, if the stock price should climb to $60 per share, each convertible bond would have a market value of approximately $3,000 (50 shares of stock at $60 per share) even though the face value of the bond remains unchanged at $1,000.

On the downside, convertible bonds nearly always provide an investor with lower returns from interest income compared to the returns that could be earned from regular bonds. Corporations in large part are influenced to issue convertible bonds because of the opportunity to borrow money at a lower interest expense. A firm may be able to issue regular 20-year maturity bonds with an interest coupon of 6 percent at the same time it can issue convertible bonds with similar maturity and an interest coupon of only 4 percent. Investors are willing to accept a lower interest rate on a convertible bond because of the possibility that they will benefit from a large increase in the value of the underlying stock into which the bond can be converted. Investors who favor convertible bonds over regular bonds accept reduced interest income in return for the possibility of a larger capital gain. Keep in mind that most convertible bonds are unsecured debt. That is, they are debentures or subordinated debentures that can subject an investor to substantial risk from loss of principal in the event the issuer gets into financial difficulty.

3 U.S. Government and Municipal Bonds

The federal government, federal agencies, states, counties, and cities issue a wide variety of high-quality bonds. Hundreds of billions of dollars worth of these securities are issued each year as governments borrow to support deficit spending and refinance previous debt being redeemed. U.S. government bonds enjoy unsurpassed credit quality, while most municipal bonds allow investors to earn tax-exempt interest income. U.S. government and municipal bonds have many of the same investment characteristics as corporate bonds.

U.S. government and municipal securities offer an alternative to individual investors who primarily seek current income. These debt securities are substitutes for certificates of deposit, corporate bonds, and several investment products offered by life insurance companies. Government and municipal bonds are very similar to corporate bonds described in the previous chapter. Corporate, U.S. government, and municipal securities represent debt and generally require fixed interest payments, a specific date on which the principal is to be repaid, and a legal promise on the part of the issuer to pay interest and principal. Nearly all U.S. government and municipal bonds are marketable securities that can be resold to other investors prior to maturity.

U.S. Government and municipal securities have certain characteristics that differentiate them from corporate bonds. The federal government and state and local governments have the power of taxation to support the payment of interest and principal, a guarantee that strengthens the credit quality of many of these securities. Also, certain valuable tax advantages can accrue to investors who own government securities.

How Governments Are Financed

Governments and governmental organizations typically support most of their spending with funds that are raised through taxation or the collection of fees. The U.S. government annually raises hundreds of billions of dollars with its levies on individual and business income. The federal government also earns fee income from certain services and products that it sells. States raise funds using a variety of taxes and fees. Many states are heavily dependent on sales tax revenues, while other states rely mostly on business and individual income taxes. Numerous states have chosen to levy both an income tax and a sales tax. County and municipal governments have historically relied heavily on property taxes to supply the funds they require to pay for schools, roads, and local governmental operations. Many local governments have turned to sales taxes to supplement revenues from property taxes.

A government has no need to search for additional funds if it is able to collect enough in taxes and fees to pay for all of its current spending needs. As difficult as it may be to believe, governments periodically take in more money in taxes and fees than they spend. More frequently, governments operate at a deficit by spending more money than is raised from taxation and fees. A deficit means it is necessary to use reserves accumulated during past years or to borrow funds. In some instances the gap between spending and revenues represents only a small percentage of a government's overall expenditures; in other cases governments borrow to support a substantial proportion of their overall spending. Government borrowing to support a shortage of revenues, also called deficit financing, is especially prevalent during periods of weak economic activity when tax revenues decline at the same time that additional demands are made for government services. Figure 5 illustrates net borrowing by the U.S. government, corporations, and state and local governments.

Figure 5 ■ Net Borrowing in U.S. Credit Markets (1985–2001)

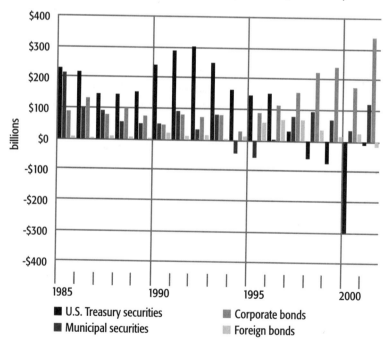

Governments cannot raise money by selling ownership units similar to the shares of common stock that are issued by business firms. Stock represents ownership of an enterprise, and governmental organizations have no owners. Thus one of the main sources of financing for businesses—selling shares of ownership—is not available to governments, which are forced to rely only on borrowing to supply the financing that normal revenues do not provide.

Governments sometimes meet their borrowing needs by arranging loans from financial institutions such as commercial banks. Most times, however, governments utilize the financial markets to issue debt securities that are purchased by individuals and institutions. The U.S. Treasury regularly announces how much it intends to borrow and then allows institutions and individuals to enter bids for the securities that are to be issued. Federal agencies, states, and cities utilize investment bankers to provide assistance in the sale of debt securities.

Why don't governments that require additional funds to support current or expected spending simply raise taxes and avoid the need to borrow? The major reason is that politicians are concerned voters will retaliate against elected officials who propose and approve tax increases. One justification for government borrowing stems from the substantial amount of government spending that pays for long-lived assets such as bridges, buildings, roads, schools, and military equipment that will be utilized for many years. Most governments are unwilling or unable to levy the huge amount of taxes that would be required to pay up front for all these items. Regardless of the reasons, government borrowing creates investment opportunities for individual investors.

U.S. Government and Federal Agency Bonds

The United States government issues many types of high-quality debt securities with a wide range of maturities. A large portion of U.S. government debt is issued and backed by the full faith and credit of the U.S. government. Federal agencies issue bonds with promises that are considered somewhat less secure than direct obligations of the U.S. Treasury. Bonds issued by federal agencies are often called *agency issues* or *federal agency issues* to distinguish these securities from direct obligations of the U.S. Treasury.

U.S. Treasury and federal agency securities are issued in denominations from $1,000 to $100,000. The more popular issues among individual investors are issued in denominations of up to $25,000. Most government bonds that are issued with maturities of over a year pay semiannual interest. As with corporate bonds, the amount of the semiannual payments is dependent on a bond's face value and coupon rate. Purchase a $10,000 face amount U.S. Treasury bond that has a 6-percent coupon rate and you will receive annual interest of $600 in the form of two $300 semiannual payments. Treasury securities with original maturities of a year or less are issued at discounts from face value and do not pay semiannual interest. Income is earned between the price paid and the face value received at maturity.

Fixed interest payments cause the market values of outstanding U.S. government securities to be influenced by market rates of interest. For example, an outstanding government bond with a 6-percent coupon that pays $60 in annual interest will have a market price above its face value when the interest rate on new government bonds with a similar maturity is only 5 percent. A government bond with a 4-percent coupon will trade at a price below its face value when market interest rates are considerably higher than 4 percent. Because government securities have lit-

> **Tip** Interest income from U.S. government securities including U.S. Treasury bonds and U.S. savings bonds is not taxable by state and local governments. This makes these securities particularly attractive for individuals who reside in states and cities with high income tax rates. This feature is of less interest to individuals who reside in states such as Florida and Nevada that do not levy an income tax.

tle credit risk (risk that promised payments will not be made in a timely manner), the degree to which these bonds fluctuate in value is mostly a function of a security's maturity length and changes in market interest rates.

The high credit quality of U.S. government bonds allows both the Treasury and federal agencies to borrow at relatively low interest rates compared to the rates paid by private borrowers. The government's low cost of borrowing may save you some taxes, but it also means that U.S. government securities will provide a lower return than is available on comparable corporate bonds. The low return on government securities may be at least partly compensated for by a potential tax advantage. All obligations of the U.S. Treasury and some obligations of federal agencies pay interest that is not subject to taxation by state and local authorities. Investors who reside in states such as California and New York that levy high personal income tax rates can achieve noticeable tax savings by choosing to invest in U.S. government securities.

Types of U.S. Government Bonds

All U.S. government bonds are not identical. In fact, the U.S. government and its agencies issue a variety of debt securities that are available for purchase by individual investors. Many novice investors are familiar with U.S. savings bonds, but these are actually unique investments and much different from other U.S. government debt. One thing is common to all U.S. government debt, however, and that is a high degree of safety of principal. In other respects, investments collectively referred to as government debt exhibit substantial differences.

U.S. Savings Bonds

U.S. savings bonds are unlike any other direct obligations of the U.S. Treasury. These popular investments are not marketable, meaning that they cannot be purchased from or resold to other investors. U.S. savings bonds can be purchased online or from agents of the U.S. Treasury and can only be liquidated by having the bonds redeemed by agents of the U.S. Treasury. Investors have a choice of holding the bonds until maturity or of redeeming the bonds prior to maturity. Series EE savings bonds are issued at 50 percent of face value and accrue variable interest that is paid when the bonds are redeemed. The interest paid on Series EE bonds is calculated as 90 percent of the yield on 5-year Treasury Bonds. These bonds offer potential tax advantages for families with children who will some day attend college. Series HH savings bonds are less familiar and less popular than Series EE savings bonds. Series HH bonds are issued at face value and pay semiannual interest payments and can only be obtained in exchange for Series EE bonds. Exchanging a matured Series EE bond for a Series HH bond has the advantage of deferring an investor's tax liability. Recently introduced Series I savings bonds offer a third option for investors who are concerned about unexpected inflation as well as safety of principal. Series I bonds are issued at face value and pay interest that is adjusted each May and November for changes in the consumer price index. Unlike Series EE and HH bonds that pay a

> **Tip** Current yields and comprehensive information about U.S. savings bonds are available at website *www.savingsbonds.gov.* Series EE and Series I savings bonds may be purchased directly on the web using a credit card for payment. This method of purchase offers the possibility of earning frequent flier points or other rewards at the same time it allows the buyer to delay parting with cash until the credit card payment due date.

variable rate linked to 5-year U.S. Treasury securities, Series I bonds pay a fixed rate plus an inflation rate adjustment. An increase in the inflation rate causes these bonds to pay an increased rate of interest. Decreases in inflation result in Series I bonds paying a reduced rate of interest. Somewhat surprisingly, individuals can use a credit card to purchase U.S. savings bonds via the Internet.

U.S. Treasury Securities

The U.S. Treasury offers transferable debt securities in three maturity classes: bills, notes, and bonds. U.S. Treasury bills are short-term securities issued in minimum denominations of $10,000, and in $5,000 multiples thereafter. Treasury bills with maturities of 13 weeks (91 days) and 26 weeks (182 days) are auctioned each Monday. All Treasury bills are issued on the Thursday following the date of sale, and bills mature on a Thursday.

Treasury bills are auctioned at a discount from face value and do not make regular interest payments like most bonds. Investors who purchase the bills earn interest income equal to the difference between the price they pay and the face value that is paid at maturity (or the amount that is received in a sale prior to maturity). The discounted price replaces semiannual interest payments that are received from owning most fixed income securities. The greater the difference between the face value and the price you pay for a Treasury bill, the more interest income you will earn. Suppose you purchased a $10,000 13-week bill at a price of $9,850. Hold the bill for the full 13 weeks and you will earn interest income equal to the amount you receive at redemption ($10,000) less the amount you paid ($9,850), or $150. Treasury bills always sell at a discount from face value.

The market for U.S. Treasury bills is very active, meaning the securities can be easily and inexpensively sold prior to their scheduled maturity. At the time a Treasury bill is purchased there is no way to determine the exact price that will be received if you decide to sell the bill prior to maturity. You can, however, generally expect to receive a price that is between the bill's face value and the price you paid. In other words, it is unlikely that you will lose money on an investment in U.S. Treasury bills. Treasury bills are scheduled for redemption in such a short time that the securities do not fluctuate much in price.

Like Treasury bills, U.S. Treasury notes and bonds are direct obligations of the U.S. government. In other words, there is virtually no risk of not being paid the promised interest and principal. U.S. Treasury notes have original maturities of from 2 to 10 years, and U.S. Treasury bonds have original maturities of over

Tip Although U.S. Treasury securities are considered rock solid from the standpoint of credit quality, the market value of long-term U.S. Treasuries can exhibit large swings as interest rates change. Thus, these securities can subject you to substantial risk in the event you may be required to sell the bonds prior to maturity.

10 years. Two- and three-year notes are issued in minimum denominations of $5,000, and notes of 4 years and above are issued in $1,000 denominations. Two-year Treasury notes are auctioned near the end of each month, and all other notes and bonds are auctioned every 3 months. Notes and bonds are issued at face value and, like corporate bonds, pay semiannual interest that is determined by the face value and the coupon rate, respectively. Interest payments on a note or bond remain the same from the date of issue to the date of redemption.

A limited number of Treasury securities are subject to early redemption, although call provisions on Treasuries are much more favorable to investors compared to call provisions on corporate debt. Most Treasury securities, including all Treasury notes, cannot be redeemed early. Treasury bonds that are callable can only be redeemed 5 years prior to their scheduled maturities. This compares to corporate bonds that are generally callable from 5 to 10 years following the date of issue.

U.S. Treasury notes and bonds may be purchased from the Federal Reserve on the date of issue or they may be bought from other investors in the secondary market. Brokerage firms and commercial banks can facilitate the purchase of Treasuries for you in either market, and the commission is nominal. Choosing to buy Treasury securities directly allows you to bypass a brokerage company and the accompanying commission. No fee is charged when purchasing Treasury securities directly from the Federal Reserve and the process is uncomplicated. First, you must open an account by completing a one-page form that includes your social security number and information about the account to which you want the Treasury to credit interest and principal payments. After opening an account you can participate in an auction.

Most individuals who purchase Treasury bills directly from

the Federal Reserve do so with a noncompetitive tender, which means they agree to accept the average yield at which a particular issue of bills is auctioned. A noncompetitive tender allows the direct purchase of Treasury bills without the worry of having to bid in an auction. For information on direct purchases of Treasury securities, write or visit your local Federal Reserve bank or write: Bureau of the Public Debt, Division of Customer Services, 300 13th Street S.W., Washington, D. C. 20239-0001. Alternatively, you can visit the U.S. Treasury website at http://www.publicdebt.treas.gov.

Federal Agency Issues

A number of federal agencies borrow enormous amounts of money by selling notes and bonds to investors. Federal agency debt is generally considered high quality even though only a few of these debt issues are fully guaranteed by the U.S. government. Most financial analysts believe the Treasury would step in to aid a financially troubled agency although its intervention isn't guaranteed. Without an explicit guarantee by the U.S. government, federal agency issues are generally judged slightly less creditworthy than bonds issued by the U.S. Treasury. The difference in credit risk causes federal agency issues to provide somewhat higher returns than U.S. Treasury bonds.

The pass-through security is one unusual type of agency debt that has achieved great popularity among institutional and individual investors alike. Pass-through securities have special features that make them quite different from ordinary bonds and notes. Ginnie Mae is one of several federal agencies that issue pass-through securities. To provide mortgage lenders with additional funds, Ginnie Mae assembles pools of Veterans Administration and Federal Housing Administration insured mortgages that it packages and sells to investors as separate securities called

Ginnie Mae pass-throughs. Ginnie Mae collects and passes through on a monthly basis the principal and interest payments it receives on mortgages that secure the pass-through securities. The underlying VA and FHA mortgages in these pools are insured and Ginnie Mae guarantees principal and interest on the pass-throughs. The guaranteed mortgages and the added guarantee by Ginnie Mae make these pass-throughs very high-quality debt.

The successful introduction of Ginnie Mae pass-throughs in the mid 1960s spawned new types of Ginnie Mae securities in addition to the packaging and sale of pass-throughs from other federal agencies and from private institutions involved in the mortgage business. Freddie Mac and Fannie Mae are two other major issuers of pass-through securities.

Pass-through securities are popular with investors because of the high return they provide relative to other fixed income investments. In addition, the agencies' guarantees relieve investors of concern about possible nonpayment of interest or principal. The problem with pass-through securities from an investor's point of view is the uncertainty regarding the size of monthly payments that will be received. Payments made to the holder of a pass-through are subject to large variations from one month to the next. Ginnie Mae, Freddie Mac, and Fannie Mae pass through whatever payments are received from borrowers, including principal payments. Borrowers sometimes repay loans early, meaning that the holder of a pass-through may unexpectedly receive a large principal payment sooner than expected. Mortgage prepayments are particularly heavy when market rates of interest are low and many homeowners choose to refinance their mortgages. Refinancing causes investors holding pass-through securities to have principal returned at a time when reinvested funds will earn a low return.

Municipal Bonds

Although most people think of a municipality as a town or city, reference to municipal bonds is generally used in a generic sense that includes bonds issued by a city, county, state, or certain other public districts. Essentially, this category of securities includes virtually all bonds issued by a domestic government or government agency that is not associated with the federal government. Municipal bonds are issued in order to raise funds to pay for bridges, courthouses, toll roads, schools, water and sewage systems, sports stadiums, airports, public office buildings, and a thousand other things that state and local governments require. The revenues from projects financed with municipal bonds are sometimes used to guarantee the payment of interest and principal. Other municipal bonds enjoy a more secure guarantee of repayment from tax revenues.

Municipal bonds are issued in $5,000 denominations and multiples thereof. These securities are available in several classifications and a wide variety of maturities. Maturities on newly issued municipal bonds range from several months to 30 years and more. Zero-coupon municipal bonds are issued at large discounts from face value but pay no periodic interest. A limited number of municipal bonds pay interest only after being outstanding for a specified number of years. By and large, however, municipal bonds are similar to the majority of corporate and government bonds; that is, most municipal bonds are issued at face value with a coupon rate that establishes semiannual interest payments. Following the issue date a municipal bond trades among investors in the secondary market at a price that causes the bond's return to be competitive with newly issued municipal bonds of similar risk and maturity.

Types of Municipal Bonds

Municipal bonds are frequently classified according to the guarantee provided to bondholders. *General obligation bonds*, also called *GOs*, are backed by the full faith and credit of the issuing government entity. For example, a general obligation bond issued by the state of Nevada has the full taxing power of the state behind the promise of repayment. Likewise, a GO issued by the village of Rushville, Indiana, has the local government's taxing authority to guarantee that bondholders will be paid. Although a government's taxing power is generally considered to be strong financial backing for a debt, not all general obligation municipal bonds are equally creditworthy.

A second broad category of municipal securities, called *revenue bonds*, is guaranteed by revenues from the project the bonds are issued to finance. For example, a hospital authority may issue revenue bonds to pay for a major hospital expansion. Payments of interest and principal on the bonds are guaranteed by the hospital authority and come only from hospital revenues. Suppose a city issues bonds to raise the funds to finance an expansion of its water and sewer system. The bonds are revenue bonds if principal and interest on the bonds are to be paid only from water and sewage fees charged to users of the system. These same securities would be classified as general obligation bonds if interest and principal are guaranteed by the full taxing power of the city, even though funds raised from the issue are devoted to water and sewage facilities.

Ownership of revenue bonds generally entails more risk than ownership of general obligation bonds, although any comparison must be made on a case-by-case basis. For example, revenue bonds issued to help finance a city-owned electric utility may be of higher credit quality than general obligation bonds issued by a small town with a weak tax base. Although such exceptions exist, general obligation bonds, especially GOs of states and financially strong cities, are generally considered to be of very high credit quality. Most individual investors judge the credit risk of these securities by relying on the ratings of bond rating companies.

Many municipal revenue bonds and a limited number of general obligation bonds are insured by outside firms. The insurance guarantees that the insurer will pay interest and principal in the event the issuer is unable to fulfill the terms of the issue. A municipal authority may purchase insurance from a private source when interest savings from selling a higher quality bond issue are greater than the premium charged by the insurance company. Insured bonds carry higher bond ratings and lower interest rates because investors can look to payment from the insurance company if the issuer is unable to pay interest or principal. Several insurance companies guarantee municipal debt. Large commercial banks also sometimes guarantee debt.

The Tax Advantage of Municipal Bonds

Investors typically purchase municipal bonds for a single reason—to earn tax-free interest income. Interest payments made by the majority of municipal bonds are exempt from federal taxation and may also be exempt from state and local taxation. The tax exemption of municipal bond interest is primarily of interest to individual investors who pay relatively high rates of federal taxes on their income. Individuals who pay modest income taxes should generally avoid buying municipal bonds.

The exemption of municipal bond interest from state and local income taxes depends upon the state law in an investor's state of residence. Most states do not tax interest income from municipal bonds issued within the states. For example, Georgia does not tax its residents' incomes that are derived from inter-

> **Tip**
> Municipal bonds are nearly always inappropriate investments for tax-sheltered retirement accounts. Interest received from municipal bonds is generally tax exempt so there is no need to shelter the income from taxation in a retirement account. Corporate bonds paying taxable income are generally better suited for retirement accounts.

est payments on municipal bonds issued within Georgia. However, Georgia does tax the interest income from municipal bonds issued outside the state. A limited number of states exempt from taxation all interest income received from municipal securities, and a few states tax all municipal bond interest.

The tax exemption extended to municipal bond interest results in municipalities being able to borrow money at relatively low interest rates. For example, at a time when high quality corporate bonds provide returns of 6 percent and U.S. Treasury securities are returning 5 percent, high-quality municipal bonds may offer returns of only 4 percent. Municipalities are able to borrow at relatively low interest rates because of the tax-exempt interest payments.

Not all municipal bonds pay interest that is completely free of taxes. Municipal bonds issued to finance "nonessential" expenditures (as classified by the federal government) pay interest that may be subject to the federal alternative minimum tax (AMT). The alternative minimum tax was enacted to ensure that individuals who take advantage of tax shelters and "loopholes" pay their fair share of taxes. An increasing number of individuals are impacted by the alternative minimum tax, so it is worthwhile to consider whether you should own municipal bonds paying interest subject to the AMT.

A relatively small number of municipal bonds pay taxable interest. Tax reform in the mid 1980s restricted the kinds of projects that municipal issuers are permitted to finance with tax-exempt debt. For example, proceeds from tax-exempt bonds can no longer be used to pay for convention centers and sports complexes. Municipalities sometimes decide to go forward with bond issues to finance restricted projects even though the bonds they issue will pay taxable interest. The taxable interest, in turn, will cause municipal borrowers to pay substantially higher interest rates on the debt compared to the rate they would pay if the interest payments were not subject to taxes.

Are Municipal Bonds for You?

The question of whether to invest in municipal bonds boils down to two factors: Do fixed-income investments of any type fit your investment goals, and does your tax status justify the ownership of tax-exempt bonds? If fixed income investments do not fit your needs, then municipal bonds should be avoided regardless of the tax savings. Likewise, if you pay a relatively low federal tax rate it is generally wise to avoid municipal bonds and choose some other fixed income investment with a higher return.

Suppose you have a choice of investing in a taxable corporate bond that provides a return of 8 percent or a tax-exempt munic-

Tip

A paper loss on a municipal bond (i.e., the current market price of the bond is below the purchase price) creates a tax-saving opportunity. Selling the bond and reinvesting the proceeds in a similar bond creates a realized loss that reduces taxable income. At the same time the replacement bond continues interest payments that are exempt from income taxes.

ipal bond with a return of 6 percent. If you pay no taxes the choice is obvious; you should choose the corporate bond that offers a higher return on both a before-tax and an after-tax basis. If you pay combined federal and state taxes at a rate of 40 percent, you should choose the municipal bond with a return of 6 percent because paying taxes on interest from the corporate bond would result in an after-tax return of only 4.8 percent. Returns from tax-exempt and taxable bonds can be compared using the following formula:

$$\text{Tax Equivalent Yield} = \frac{\text{Tax-Free Yield}}{1 - \text{Tax Rate}}$$

Assume you pay federal taxes at a rate of 30 percent and must choose between the two bonds just discussed. The tax equivalent yield of the 6-percent municipal bond is equal to 6 percent divided by .70, or 8.57 percent. In other words, the 6-percent municipal bond provides a return that is comparable to a taxable return of 8.57 percent. Because the municipal bond's tax equivalent yield is higher than the return you could earn on the taxable bond (8.57 percent versus 8 percent), you should choose the municipal bond. Viewed from the opposite perspective, the after-tax return earned on the corporate bond will be lower than the return provided by the tax-exempt municipal bond. You can make a wise choice between taxable and nontaxable returns only after making this comparison. The information in Figure 6 (p. 58) allows you to determine your marginal income tax rate based on the amount of your taxable income. Keep in mind that your overall marginal rate is a combination of both federal and state taxes.

Figure 6 ■ Determining Your Marginal Federal Income Tax Rate (Tax Year 2003)

Married Individuals Filing Jointly

Taxable Income	Marginal Tax Rate
$ 14,000 or less	10 percent
$ 14,000 to $ 56,800	15 percent
$ 56,800 to $114,650	25 percent
$114,650 to $174,700	28 percent
$174,700 to $311,950	33 percent
over $311,950	35 percent

Single

Taxable Income	Marginal Tax Rate
$ 7,000 or less	10 percent
$ 7,000 to $28,400	15 percent
$ 28,400 to $68,800	25 percent
$ 68,800 to $143,500	28 percent
$ 143,500 to $311,950	33 percent
over $311,950	35 percent

4 Bond Valuation and Yields

The size, timing, and certainty of future cash flows are the main determinants of any investment's current value. The cash flows to most bondholders consist of fixed semiannual interest payments plus the principal that is returned at maturity. Investors determine whether a bond is properly valued by comparing the bond's yield, or rate of return, with the yields that are available on competing investments. Several measures of yields are utilized to evaluate the return from owning a bond.

Investments are valuable for the cash they are expected to provide to their owners. Common stocks pay dividends and are eventually converted into cash when shares are sold; rental housing produces rental income and cash from the eventual sale of the structure; and although gold bullion doesn't produce any current income, a cash payment is received when the bullion is eventually sold. Bonds deliver fixed semiannual interest payments that are particularly prized by investors who seek current income. A bond's final cash payment is the money that is received when the bond is redeemed by the issuer or sold to another investor. Some investments (including certain bonds) promise relatively small or no current interest payments and are valued only for the cash they are expected to produce when they are sold. In general, an investment is more valuable the greater the amount of cash it returns, the sooner the cash is to be received, and the more certain it is that the cash receipts will occur as expected.

Bonds are valued in the same manner as all other investment assets: investors estimate the amounts of the cash flows they expect to receive, when the cash flows will occur, and, based on the cost, the rate of return the investment is expected to provide. Bonds are easier to value than most investments because both the amounts and the timing of a bond's cash payments are known. Most other investments—including stocks, coin collections, options, and real estate—require investors to estimate the size and timing of cash payments. Estimates are often no more than educated guesses that all too frequently prove to be wildly inaccurate. Cash flows from bonds are much easier to determine.

How Assets Are Valued

In formal financial terminology an asset should sell at a price that equals the present value of the investment's expected cash flows. The present value of an investment is calculated by discounting the expected cash flows (that is, reducing or penalizing the cash flows because you must wait for the payments) at an appropriate rate. Choosing an appropriate discount rate is a subjective judgment that is primarily based on the yields that are currently available on similar investments. Suppose you are considering the purchase of an investment that will return a single payment of $5,000 in one year. No further cash payments are promised or expected. If you are absolutely certain that the payment will take place as promised, what is the maximum price you should offer for the investment?

The Importance of Timing

The amount you should pay now for $5,000 to be received in one year depends upon the rate of return you expect the asset to provide. If you are willing to put your money away for a year without earning any return, you should be willing to offer $5,000 for the asset. In other words, you pay $5,000 now for the right to receive $5,000 in one year. The rate of return on this transaction is zero because the investment returns no profit. Paying a price less than $5,000 will produce a profit, so you will earn a positive return. The lower the price you pay, the higher the return you will earn. Stated another way, the higher the return you demand from the asset, the lower the price you should offer. For example, if you have decided to accept no less than a 10-percent annual return, you should pay a maximum price of $4,546 today for the right to receive the $5,000 payment in one year. Paying $4,546 now for $5,000 in one year will yield a profit of $454 that translates to a return of exactly 10 percent. Conversely, paying more than $4,546 will produce a return of less than 10 percent.

Now suppose the single $5,000 payment is to occur at the end of two years rather than at the end of one year. Expecting the same 10-percent annual return means you should pay substantially less than $4,546 to acquire the investment because you are required to wait an additional year before receiving the same amount of cash. To earn an annual return of 10 percent from the investment that pays $5,000 in two years, you would have to purchase the asset at a price of $4,132. If the $5,000 payment is not to occur until the end of three years, you can earn a 10-percent annual return only if you are able to purchase the investment for no more than $3,756. The longer you are required to wait for an investment's cash flows, the less the investment is worth today.

There is another consideration relative to the timing of an investment's cash flows. Investors generally expect a higher annual yield to invest their money for a longer period of time. You may decide that you will invest your money for two years only if you are rewarded with an annual return somewhat higher than the 10-percent return you expect on a one-year investment. Perhaps you feel you need an annual return of 11 percent or 12 percent because of the longer period your funds are tied up.

Figure 7 illustrates the typical relationship between yield and maturity for U.S. Treasury debt. In financial jargon the relationship between these two variables is known as a *yield curve.* The upward-sloping yield curve demonstrates that Treasury securities with longer maturities provide investors with higher yields. The same direct relationship between yield and maturity

Figure 7 ■ U.S. Treasury Yield Curve (Late 2002)

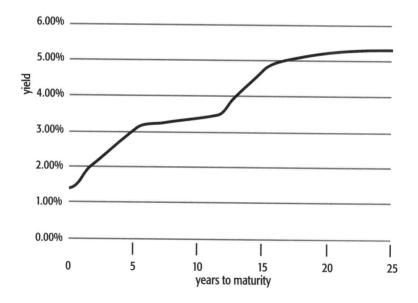

length nearly always applies for other types of debt. For example, short-term corporate bonds typically provide lower annual returns than long-term corporate bonds.

The Importance of Certainty

An asset's value is also influenced by investor confidence that the asset's expected cash flows will occur as promised. Financial theory assumes that investors tend to avoid risky assets unless they expect to receive extra compensation in the form of higher yields. Thus, the less certain you are about the amount and timing of an investment's cash flows, the higher the rate of return you are likely to demand from the investment. A higher rate of return will be earned only if you are able to acquire an investment for a lower price. Suppose an investment is expected to pay $5,000 in one year but the amount of the payment is not absolutely certain and there is some possibility you will receive less than $5,000. The lack of certainty regarding the amount of cash you will receive is likely to cause you to commit money to the investment only if you expect an annual return of more than 10 percent. If you are willing to pay $4,546 for a certain payment of $5,000 in one year, you should pay less than $4,546 for a less-than-certain $5,000 in

Tip Investors who worry about the health of the economy often seek the safety of a U.S. government guarantee that they will receive promised interest payments and the return of principal. As a result, the spread in yields between U.S. Treasury securities and corporate bonds tends to widen during periods of economic decline when investors become more concerned about safety of principal than about size of the return they earn. This is often the best time to invest in high quality corporate debt securities.

one year. Not surprisingly, U.S. Treasury bonds with certain payments typically promise a much smaller return than bonds issued by companies of poor financial standing.

How Bonds Are Valued

Suppose you are considering the purchase of a $1,000 principal, 5-percent coupon bond that has 4 years remaining to maturity. Purchase the bond and you are promised eight $25 semiannual interest payments in addition to a $1,000 principal payment at the end of 4 years. No matter what price you pay to purchase the bond, you will receive exactly nine cash payments if you hold the bond to maturity. The size and timing of each payment are stipulated in the bond issue's indenture agreement.

In order to determine whether to purchase the bond you must first establish the rate of return that you consider to be satisfactory. The rate is used to discount the promised cash flows and establish the maximum price you should pay for the bond. Figure 8 indicates the appropriate price you should pay for the 4-year, 5-percent coupon bond depending on whether you expect to earn an annual return of 2 percent, 4 percent, 6 percent or 8 percent.

Each column lists a series of discounted values that represent each of the semiannual interest payments and the principal for one of four rates of return. The bond value at each return is equal to the sum of the discounted values for the nine cash payments that you would receive as a bondholder. According to the data in Figure 8, the bond is worth no more than $964.89 if you determine that you should earn an annual return of at least 6 percent for the 4-year holding period. If you are satisfied with an annual return of 2 percent, you can afford to pay $1,114.79 to acquire the bond.

The return that you should expect to earn from the bond will depend upon the return that you are able to earn from other investments of similar risk and maturity. For example, if the bond noted above is guaranteed by the full faith and credit of the U.S. government, you should expect to earn an annual return equal to the return that is currently available on other four-year U.S. government bonds. If a corporation of substantial financial strength issued the bond, you should be able to purchase the security for a price that allows you to earn a return that is somewhat higher than the yield on U.S. government

Figure 8 ■ Required Rates of Return and Bond Payment Values ($1,000 principal, 5-percent coupon, 4-year maturity)

| Payment | Annual Return You Expect to Earn | | | |
	2 Percent	4 Percent	6 Percent	8 Percent
$25	$ 24.75	$ 24.51	$ 24.27	$ 24.04
25	24.51	24.03	23.56	23.12
25	24.26	23.56	22.88	22.22
25	24.02	23.10	22.21	21.37
25	23.79	22.64	21.56	20.55
25	23.55	22.20	20.94	19.76
25	23.32	21.76	20.33	19.00
25	23.09	21.34	19.74	18.27
1,000	923.50	853.50	789.40	730.70
Bond Price*	$1,114.79	$1,036.64	$964.89	$899.03

*The price at which a $1,000 principal, 5-percent coupon, 4-year maturity bond must sell to provide the yield indicated at the top of each column.

bonds. The promise is a little weaker and the return you earn should be a little higher than on U.S. government bonds.

The Yields from Bond Investments

A bond is a relatively simple investment: you pay a lump sum to acquire an asset that makes fixed semiannual interest payments and eventually returns its face value. You know how much money is required to purchase the bond, and you know the exact timing and amounts of the cash payments you will receive. Pretty simple, huh? Not necessarily. Several measures of return can be quoted for the same bond and the measures are each likely to produce different returns! Suppose a broker calls to tout a bond that she says will provide a yield of 6 percent. Exactly what type of yield is the broker quoting? It would seem that at any point in time there should be a single measure of a bond's return. Actually, one or more of five measures of yield are used to price bonds. To protect yourself against being hoodwinked by an unscrupulous broker intent on convincing you to purchase an overvalued bond, you need to understand each of the various measures of yield and when each of the measures is appropriate to use.

Nominal Yield

Nominal yield is a bond's coupon rate—a measure of annual return based on the annual interest payment and the bond's face value. Nominal yield is established at the time a bond is issued and remains unchanged until the bond is redeemed. Nominal yield is a function only of a bond's face value and annual interest payment. Neither of these changes from the bond's issue date to the redemption date. Nominal yield is not affected by changes in market interest rates or changes in the market value of the bond. Nominal yield is important because it is a reflection of the annual dollar amount of interest that a buyer will receive. Like the coupon rate and face value, the nominal yield of a bond remains constant until a bond is redeemed. Nominal yield is computed as:

$$\text{Nominal Yield} = \frac{\text{Annual Interest Payment}}{\text{Face Value of Bond}}$$

Although a bond's nominal yield is valuable for determining the amount of annual interest that will be paid, it is not an accurate measure of the bondholder's annual return unless the bond is purchased at face value and redeemed at face value. Suppose a bond with an 8-percent coupon is scheduled to mature in 5 years. If you purchase the bond at a price equal to its face value and hold the bond to maturity, you will earn an annual return of 8 percent, the nominal yield. If you pay any price other than face value, however, you will earn an annual return different from the nominal yield. Likewise, if you purchase the bond at face value and later resell it at a price other than face value you will have earned an annual return different from the bond's nominal yield. Nominal yield is frequently used to identify a bond issue ("8 percents of 09" refers to a bond issue with an 8-percent coupon and a maturity date of 2009) and to determine the dollar amount of annual interest a bond pays.

Tip

Bonds with long maturities are subject to large changes in market value. A given change in the market rate of interest has a much greater impact on bonds with long maturities than on bonds with short maturities.

Current Yield

Current yield is a frequently used measure of return that is calculated using a bond's annual interest payment and current market price. Current yield is computed as:

$$\text{Current Yield} = \frac{\text{Annual Interest Income}}{\text{Current Bond Price}}$$

Suppose a bond with a principal amount of $1,000 and a coupon rate of 9 percent currently sells at a price of $950. The bond's current yield is equal to the annual interest of $90 (9 percent of $1,000) divided by the current price of $950, or 9.47 percent. The current yield is always higher than the coupon rate, or nominal yield, when a bond sells at a discount from face value. If the bond had been selling at a price higher than $1,000, the current yield would be below the coupon rate of 9 percent. Current yield is equal to the nominal yield only when a bond sells at par (as it often does on the date of issue).

Current yield is simple to calculate, easy to understand, and frequently published in the financial section of major daily newspapers. This measure of yield is of interest to individuals who invest primarily for current income. The problem with using current yield as a measure of the annual return you will earn from purchasing a bond is that it does not take into account a possible or likely change in a bond's market value. In the example noted above, current yield does not account for the fact that the bond can be purchased for $950 and will eventually be redeemed for its $1,000 face value. The $50 gain is not a major consideration if the bond matures in 30 years. If the bond is scheduled to mature in only 2 years, however, the current yield calculation omits a substantial amount of annual income ($25 for each of 2 years) from a gain in value that will accrue to the owner. In fact, the great disadvantage of current yield as a measure of return is that it does not take into account any future change in the market value of a bond. Without taking price changes into account, current yield understates the annual return of a bond that sells at a price below face value and overstates the annual return of a bond that sells at a price above face value. Whenever a bond sells at a price other than face value, current yield provides an incomplete picture of the return you are likely to earn because it omits the effect of changes in the price of the bond.

Yield to Maturity

Yield to maturity (YTM) is the most frequently used measure of a bond's return. If a broker quotes a bond's yield but fails to identify which particular version of yield is being used, the chances are you are being provided with the bond's yield to maturity. The calculation for yield to maturity is more useful than the nominal yield or the current yield because YTM includes both interest income and expected changes in the market value of a bond from the current date until maturity. If a bond sells at a premium to face value, yield to maturity takes into account the gradual reduction in the market value of the bond during the years until maturity. This reduction in value offsets a portion of the interest income the bondholder will receive. When a bond sells at a discount from face value the yield to maturity accounts for the gradual increase in the value of the bond that will take place as the bond approaches face value at maturity. The gain in value combined with interest income causes the yield to maturity of a discounted bond to be higher than either the nominal yield or the current yield. Only when a bond sells at face value and interest is the only source of income is yield to maturity equal to current yield.

Suppose a bond with a 5-percent coupon is scheduled for

> **Tip**
>
> Buying municipal bonds at a discount in the secondary market will result in your being required to report capital gains as the bond appreciates in value. Thus, the quoted yield to maturity at the time you purchase the bonds will overstate the after-tax return you will earn from owning the bonds. Only interest income on municipal bonds is exempt from federal income taxation.

redemption at its $1,000 face value at maturity in 10 years. The bond was issued at face value several years ago, but subsequent increases in market interest rates cause the bond to be priced currently at only $850. At the current market price of $850 the bond's nominal yield is 5 percent (as stated on the bond) and the current yield is $50 ÷ $850, or 5.88 percent. Purchase the bond at its current price of $850 and you will earn an annual return of 5.88 percent exclusive of any change in the price of the bond. If, however, you purchase the bond at its discounted price and hold the security for 10 years, you will earn an additional $150 because the issuer will eventually pay $1,000 to redeem a bond you bought for $850. The $150 extra profit averages $15 for each year of your 10-year holding period.

The current yield calculation can be improved upon by adding the $15 average annual gain to each year's $50 interest income. Including changes in value you will earn an average annual income of $65 rather than $50 as was assumed in the current yield calculation. There is another adjustment to make, however. Adding $15 of annual price appreciation as part of annual income means you should take account of the fact that your investment in the bond will increase by $15 during each year of the 10-year holding period. Your investment in the bond increases because $15 of each year's $65 total income is added to the value of the bond rather than paid to you in current income. Additions to the bond's value mean that you will have an additional amount invested in the bond during each year of the holding period. At the time you purchase the bond you invest $850 (the purchase price), and at the time the bond is redeemed you have $1,000 invested in the bond. Over the entire 10-year holding period you have an average of $925 (halfway between what you pay and what you receive) invested in the bond.

Adjusting current yield for the annual price change and your average investment in the bond produces an approximation of the bond's yield to maturity. The approximate YTM is calculated as

$$\text{Approximate Yield to Maturity (AYM)} = \frac{I + [(Pp - Pm)/n]}{(Pp + Pm)/2}$$

Where:
I is the bond's annual interest payment (in dollars)
Pp is the bond's par value (value at redemption)
Pm is the bond's current market price
n is the number of years to maturity

Substituting the appropriate data for the 5-percent coupon bond mentioned above produces an approximate yield to maturity of

$$
\begin{aligned}
\text{AYM} &= \frac{\$50 + [(\$1,000 - \$850)/10]}{(\$1,000 + \$850)/2} \\
&= \frac{\$50 + (150/10)}{\$1,850/2} \\
&= \frac{\$65}{\$925} \\
&= 7.03 \text{ percent}
\end{aligned}
$$

The large differences between the bond's nominal yield (5 percent), current yield (5.88 percent), and yield to maturity (7.03 percent) illustrate why a single measure of a bond's yield can prove misleading and result in faulty investment decisions. Considering only the current yield for this bond would cause you to underestimate the return you would earn from buying the bond and holding it to maturity. Thus, you might pass on an investment that actually provides a very competitive return. The opposite situation would exist if you were quoted the current yield on a bond selling at a large premium to face value.

It is important to remember that yield to maturity assumes a bond will be purchased at its current market price and held to final maturity. If you anticipate that the bond will be sold prior to maturity, yield to maturity is an important statistic but is unlikely to provide an exact measure of the return you will earn. In fact, if you later sell the bond at a price that is significantly different from the face value, the annual return you earn will be much different than the yield to maturity that was calculated at the time the bond was purchased.

Another assumption of the yield to maturity can be misleading: If you expect to be reinvesting rather than spending interest payments, YTM assumes that you will be reinvesting these payments at the rate of the yield to maturity. In the case of the bond just discussed, the YTM of 7.03 percent assumes that you will be able to reinvest each of the bond's interest payments at

Tip

Bond investments tend to do well in a weak economy when inflation rates and interest rates are relatively low. Because bond values are likely to increase when economic activity is declining, bonds provide good balance to an investor's portfolio that is heavily weighted with common stocks.

an annual rate of 7.03 percent during the term of the bond. If you discover you must reinvest at a rate lower than 7.03 percent, the yield to maturity you have been quoted overestimates your actual return on the investment. On the other hand, if you will be able to reinvest interest payments at a rate that is higher than the quoted yield to maturity, you will end up earning an overall annual return that is higher than 7.03 percent.

Yield to Call

When an issuer is expected to call (or *redeem*) a bond prior to maturity, the three measures of yield just discussed are each likely to provide an inaccurate estimate of the return the bond will provide. A debt security that is expected to be redeemed prior to maturity should be judged on the basis of the bond's yield to call, not the yield to maturity, because the bond will be redeemed prior to its scheduled maturity.

Yield to call is a measure of a bond's return that is based on the assumption that the bond will be called for redemption at a call price that will produce the lowest applicable return for bondholders. This corresponds to the lowest borrowing cost for the borrower that is calling the issue. The call price and the yield to call are particularly relevant for a bond that sells at a big premium to face value because the bond's coupon rate is substantially higher than the current market rate of interest. Suppose a bond issued several years ago with a coupon rate of 10 percent is currently selling at a price of $1,150. The bond has 10 years remaining to maturity but the issuer is permitted to call the bond at a price of $1,030 in 5 years. The bond's approximate yield to maturity is

$$\text{AYM} = \frac{\$100 + [(\$1,000 - \$1,150)/10]}{(\$1,000 + \$1,150)/2}$$

$$= \frac{\$100 - \$15}{\$1,075}$$

$$= 7.91 \text{ percent}$$

The bond will provide an approximate yield to maturity of 7.91 percent if you purchase the security at the market price of $1,150 and hold it to maturity. The problem is this bond is unlikely to remain outstanding for the full 10 years. According to the initial lending agreement, the issuer has the option of forcing bondholders to sell the bond back to the issuer at a price of $1,030 beginning 5 years prior to maturity. A slight modification in the yield to maturity formula allows you to determine the approximate annual yield you will earn if the bond is called.

$$\text{Approximate Yield to Call (AYC)} = \frac{I + [(Pc - Pm)/m]}{(Pc + Pm)/m}$$

Where:

I is the annual interest payment
Pm is the current market price of the bond
Pc is the price at which the bond can be called
m is the number of years remaining until the bond is expected to be called

The approximate yield to call for the bond discussed above is:

$$\text{AYC} = \frac{\$100 + [(\$1,030 - \$1,150)/5]}{(\$1,030 + \$1,150)/2}$$

$$= \frac{\$10 - \$24}{\$1,090}$$

$$= 6.97 \text{ percent}$$

We now have four measures of yield for the same bond. The nominal yield is 10 percent, the current yield is 8.70 percent, the yield to maturity is 7.91 percent, and the yield to call is 6.97 percent. Which is the appropriate measure of yield for an investor who owns the bond or an investor who is interested in purchasing the bond? We have already discussed that yield to maturity is generally considered a superior measure of a bond's yield compared to either the nominal yield or the current yield. Yield to maturity is also a superior measure compared to yield to call when a bond is to be held until the bond is redeemed at maturity. When a bond is likely to be called, however, the yield to call should be used to evaluate the return that will be earned from purchasing a bond. In the example above, the bond will almost certainly be called because the coupon rate of the bond is so much higher than the current market rate of interest. Thus, the yield to call is the superior measure of the bond's expected return. Purchase the bond and you will most likely earn an annual return of 6.97 percent for 5 years at which time the bond will be redeemed by the issuer. In general, yield to call should be used whenever it is lower than the yield to maturity.

The bond noted above is a prime candidate for a misleading sales presentation. A dealer holding a substantial amount of the bonds may run a newspaper advertisement that trumpets, "Earn 8.7 percent annually on an investment-quality bond." An inexperienced investor accustomed to purchasing certificates of deposit may believe that the published yield represents the

> **Tip** The market values of bonds with high coupon rates are less affected by changes in market rates of interest. In other words, when market rates of interest increase, a bond with a high coupon rate will not decline in value as much as a bond with a low coupon rate. Long-term zero-coupon bonds are most affected by changes in market rates of interest.

whole story. Without understanding that a $1,150 investment will most likely lose $120 in market value (the difference between the purchase price and call price) over a period of 5 years, the investor may be suckered into buying a bond that provides a much smaller yield than that which is advertised.

Realized Yield

The final measure of yield is the one that counts most—the yield that you will realize during the period a bond is owned. Of the five measures of yield discussed, only *realized yield* requires that you estimate two of the formula's variables—in this case, the price you will receive when the bond is liquidated and the amount of time you will hold the bond. If you plan to hold the bond until maturity or until the first call date, the realized yield will equal the yield to maturity or the yield to call, respectively. In neither instance are you called upon to make an assumption regarding the price you will receive when the bond is liquidated. If you intend to sell the bond prior to its maturity or, if applicable, before the first call date, you must estimate both the length of the holding period and the price you will receive.

The formula for calculating the approximate realized yield is similar to the previous two formulas for determining yield to maturity and yield to call, respectively.

$$\text{Approximate Realized Yield (ARY)} = \frac{I + [(Pf - Pm)/h]}{(Pf + Pm)/2}$$

> **Tip** Short-term interest rates occasionally move above long-term interest rates, but this condition is rare and usually only temporary. Short-term rates that are higher than long-term rates generally occur when lenders and borrowers expect interest rates to fall.

> **Tip**
>
> Buying bonds with borrowed money is a risky investment strategy. A subsequent increase in interest rates will result in a lower market value for your bonds at the same time that you will be required to pay a higher interest rate on the borrowed funds.

Where:

> I is the annual interest payment
> Pm is the current market price of the bond
> Pf is the estimated future selling price of the bond
> H is the number of years you expect to hold the bond

Suppose you are considering the purchase of a $1,000 face amount bond with a 7-percent coupon. The bond was issued 5 years ago with an original maturity of 15 years and is currently trading at a price of $920. You expect interest rates to fall during the next several years and believe that after a holding period of 2 years you will be able to sell the bond for at least $990. Your approximate annual realized yield during the two-year holding period is

$$\text{ARY} = \frac{\$70 + [(\$990 - \$920)/2]}{(\$990 + \$920)/2}$$

$$= \frac{\$70 + \$35}{\$955}$$

$$= 10.99 \text{ percent}$$

The relatively rapid gain that is expected in the bond's price results in a high annual yield for the 2-year holding period. The estimate for realized yield, however, is just that—an estimate—while nominal yield, current yield, yield to maturity, and yield to call are based on more substantive numbers.

5 How Bonds Are Issued and Traded

Corporate and municipal borrowers employ the services of investment banking companies to assist in planning and selling a bond issue. An investment banker generally purchases a new bond issue and then resells the bonds to individual and institutional investors. Once issued, most bonds trade in the over-the-counter market through a network of securities dealers who buy and sell bonds for their own account. Many municipal and corporate bonds rarely trade in the secondary market, which can penalize the price an investor receives when a bond is sold prior to maturity.

You can purchase bonds that are being sold as part of a new issue, or you can invest in bonds that were issued some time in the past and are currently being offered in the secondary market by dealers. Either source requires that you utilize the services of a brokerage firm or a financial institution that has access to the capital markets. Buying bonds in the secondary market has the advantage of offering a much greater selection of bonds to choose from. A wide selection is particularly important to an investor who is interested in acquiring bonds of certain issuers or bonds with specific maturities.

Bringing Bond Issues to Market

Bonds sold as part of new issues must offer investors yields that are competitive with the returns that are available on bonds being traded in the secondary market among investors. If high-quality bonds with 10-year maturities are trading among investors to yield 7 percent, new bonds of similar quality and maturities must provide a 7-percent yield in order to attract investors. Any yield lower than 7 percent would cause investors to avoid the new issue and buy bonds offered by dealers in the secondary market.

The coupon rates on new bond issues are generally established at levels that allow the bonds to be priced at or near their face values. If the yield on 10-year, high quality bonds is currently 7 percent, a new bond issue with similar characteristics is likely to have a 7-percent coupon rate that pays annual interest of $70 for each $1,000 face amount of the bond that is purchased. As market rates of interest fell throughout the 1990s and early 2000s, coupon rates on new bond issues were reduced correspondingly.

Virtually no organization has the time, the personnel, the knowledge, or the wherewithal to undertake without assistance a public bond issue. A company whose business it is to operate a large chain of grocery stores, to manufacture computers, or to explore for oil and gas will not employ the personnel or have the sales organization to sell a large bond issue by itself. The public sale of a bond issue amounting to hundreds of millions or even billions of dollars requires the assistance of a firm that understands the capital markets and has access to a large number of individual and institutional investors.

The Job of the Investment Banker

The firms that public and private borrowers regularly employ to assist them in locating willing lenders are called *investment banks*. Large broker-dealers typically have large investment banking operations that are a natural extension of their brokerage business. Other large investment banks such as JPMorgan, Morgan Stanley, and Goldman Sachs do not have a public presence in retail brokerage and are less well known outside the financial community. Investment banking firms are knowledgeable about government regulations related to securities issues and the extensive paperwork that must be completed prior to a public sale of securities. Investment banking firms have the experience and the financial knowledge to help borrowers establish the terms of a debt issue so as to minimize the cost of funds. Equally important, investment bankers are in constant touch with individual and institutional investors who are most likely to have an interest in purchasing portions of the bond issue.

Investment bankers place some debt issues directly with a single institutional lender or a small group of lenders including insurance companies, investment companies, and pension funds. These private placements are sometimes used in place of a public sale because they require less time and may entail lower expenses. Bonds issued in a private placement are unavailable to individual investors.

> **Tip**
>
> Having accounts at several brokerage firms will allow a greater selection of bonds. At any particular time different firms will have different bonds available for sale. Likewise, different firms may offer the same bond at slightly different prices. Thus, it pays to shop for bonds as well as for groceries.

A constant nightmare for an organization involved in issuing bonds (or other securities) is that some unexpected event will occur to disrupt the sale. Suppose a corporation is in the early stages of issuing $100 million worth of bonds with proceeds being used to pay for a major expansion of manufacturing capacity. The terms of the issue have been established and the selling effort to investors has just commenced. Without warning, an outbreak of hostilities in the Middle East causes interest rates to suddenly spike upward. Because interest coupons on the new bonds have already been established, the issue will be difficult to sell unless the issuer is willing to offer investors a higher yield by reducing the bonds' selling price. Lowering the bonds' selling price will increase the borrower's cost of funds and cause the issue to produce a reduced amount of financing.

To ensure that a bond issue raises the expected amount of money at a guaranteed interest cost, most borrowers enter into agreements in which the investment banker guarantees a successful sale. The guarantee consists of the investment banker buying the bonds from the issuer and then immediately reselling the securities to investors. An investment banker that guarantees a bond issue by purchasing the bonds from the issuer is said to *underwrite* the issue. An investment banker serving as an underwriter assumes the issuer's risk of being unable to sell the entire issue. If a problem in the financial markets makes it difficult to place all the bonds with investors, the investment banker rather than the issuer must absorb any losses that result.

An investment banker's profit from underwriting a bond issue comes mostly from the difference between the price paid by the investment banker and the price charged to investors. The difference between the two prices is known as the *spread* or *differential*. The size of the spread depends upon a number of variables including the size of an issue, the stability of the credit

> **Tip** It is often advantageous for individual investors to purchase bonds that are part of a new issue because all buyers, big and small, pay the same price. In addition, the issuer, not the buyers, pays all fees involved with a new issue of bonds. In other words, you won't be paying a brokerage commission when you purchase bonds that are part of a new issue.

markets, and the prominence of the issuer. Modest-size issues of $5 million to $10 million might involve a spread of $15 per $1,000 bond; large issues of $50 million and over generally involve spreads of less than $10 per $1,000 bond. An underwriting spread of $15 per bond means the investment banking firm is paying $985 for each bond being sold to the public for $1,000.

An alternative arrangement is for a borrower to employ an investment banker on a best efforts basis. In a best efforts arrangement, the investment banker is a broker that does its best to locate investors who will buy the bonds. When selling on a best efforts basis the investment banker does not actually buy the bonds for resale and, as a result, does not take the risk of being unable to sell the entire issue at the expected price. Unsold bonds from a best efforts offering are returned to the issuer, which must then locate additional financing or reduce its planned expenditures.

The Syndicate

The sale of most large bond issues involves more than a single investment banker. To spread the risk and increase the likelihood of a successful sale, investment bankers often join together in a group called a *syndicate* or *underwriting syndicate* to bid on a major bond issue. Depending upon a bond issue's size, the managing underwriter might seek the assistance of several or even dozens of other firms. When a bond issue is especially large, the underwriting syndicate will organize a selling group of smaller firms to assist in the distribution of the bonds.

All the members of an underwriting syndicate, including members of the selling group, sell the bonds at the same price. Thus, the price you pay for bonds that are part of a new issue will be the same regardless of whether you conduct business with one of the lead underwriters or some other brokerage firm that has access to securities. Many new bond issues sell out quickly, making it difficult to acquire bonds in the new issue market unless an order is placed with a member of a syndicate.

U.S. Government Issues

As discussed briefly in the previous chapter, the Federal Reserve auctions U.S. Treasury securities at regular intervals. U.S. Treasury bills with original maturities of 3 and 6 months do not make interest payments but rather are issued at a discount from face value. New issues of bills are sold to investors who agree to accept the smallest discounts. The higher the price at which the U.S. Treasury can sell bills (that is, the smaller the discount), the lower the U.S. government's borrowing cost.

U.S. Treasury notes and bonds are also sold at auction, but at

Tip Bond quotations typically include any commission. In other words, if a broker calls to tell you about a bond that offers a yield of 4.95 percent, no selling fee will be added to reduce the yield should you purchase the bond. This is in contrast to stock transactions that include a commission in addition to the quoted price.

very near their face value rather than at a large discount. Notes and bonds make semiannual interest payments, the size of which are determined by the successful bids received from investors. Investors who enter an auction for U.S. Treasury notes and bonds bid a yield (generally to two decimal places) rather than a discount. The securities are sold to investors who bid the lowest yields. Giving preference to the bids with the lowest yields allows the U.S. Treasury to minimize its cost of borrowing. Based upon the bids received and the amount of money it wishes to borrow, the U. S. Treasury determines the highest yield it will accept. Auction participants who have bid higher yields (lower prices) than the U.S. Treasury's limit will not be allocated any securities. The issue's coupon rate is set so as to establish the average price to successful bidders, equal to face value or less. In other words, notes and bonds that are part of a new issue are generally priced at a slight discount to face value.

Investors who are interested in purchasing bills, notes, or bonds, but who do not wish to submit a bid that specifies a discount or a yield, may enter a noncompetitive tender that specifies only the amount of bonds that are desired. Noncompetitive tenders do not involve a commission and are allocated on the basis of the average price of the successful bids that are received for the issue. Suppose the Treasury auctions $20 billion in bonds. If the U.S. Treasury receives $4 billion in noncompetitive tenders, $16 billion in bonds will be allocated to competitive bidders. The average yield of the bonds that are awarded to successful bidders will be paid on the bonds that are sold to investors who entered noncompetitive tenders. In practice, the difference between the highest yield and the average yield on a particular issue is generally quite small.

If you are interested in purchasing U.S. Treasury securities at auction but do not care to submit either competitive bids or

> **Tip**
>
> Bonds are typically traded in large amounts, so buying or selling only a few bonds means you are likely to be penalized with the price you pay or receive. It is generally more economical to buy shares in bond funds or unit trusts if you don't have much money to invest.

noncompetitive tenders, you may enter an order with a commercial bank or a brokerage company that will purchase the bonds in your name. A nominal fee normally charged by the financial institution that undertakes the transaction will cause a small reduction in the yield you earn.

Municipal Issues

Municipal bonds are issued through investment banking companies and selling groups to individual and institutional investors. It is common practice for a municipal borrower to sell an entire bond issue to an investment banking syndicate that quickly resells the issue in small pieces to retail buyers. The yields on a new municipal bond issue are established just prior to the time the bond issue is brought to market. Most municipal bonds are issued at or very near the face value. Last-minute changes in market interest rates may cause the managers of the issue to make slight adjustments to the coupons or the bond prices in order to make the bonds competitive. For example, a bond may be issued at a price of $990 or $995 rather than at face value. The bond's issuer will still pay face value to the bondholder at maturity.

Municipal bond issues are often comprised of *serial bonds* that mature in successive years plus one or more term bonds that make up a large proportion of the dollar amount of an issue. For example, a single municipal issue might comprise bonds that

> **Tip** A single new municipal bond issue is often comprised of a series of bonds with fifteen or twenty different maturities. New issues of these bonds generally offer great flexibility if you are interested in acquiring a bond maturing in a particular year.

mature each year for 20 years as well as a large amount of bonds that mature in 25 years. The cover from a municipal bond offering statement in Figure 9 illustrates the range of maturities that are frequently available in many municipal issues. Underwriters structure a single bond issue with different maturities in order to appeal to investors who are interested in buying bonds with specific redemption dates. The added appeal makes it easier to sell the issue and increases the likelihood that the overall interest cost is kept as low as possible.

Members of the underwriting syndicate and selling group sell new issues of municipal bonds. Salespeople at these firms contact customers and take orders prior to the actual date the bonds are issued. The demand from investors will indicate to the underwriters whether the coupons on the bonds are sufficient to sell the issue. Underwriters will sometimes reprice or adjust the yields slightly on certain maturities prior to the sale date. An investor who has placed a preliminary order to purchase a bond that has its yield adjusted downward is generally permitted to back out of the agreement without penalty.

So how can you buy bonds that are part of new municipal issues? Without scouring the financial pages you are unlikely to learn about a new issue until after the bonds have been distributed. Your best bet to participate in a new municipal bond issue is to contact several brokerage firms or commercial banks that underwrite new issues and let them know of your interest. Be certain to note any specific requirements such as whether you

Figure 9 ■ Cover from a Municipal Bond Offering Statement

NEW ISSUE

RATINGS:
S&P:AAA
(MBIA Insured)
BBB
(Underlying)
(See "MISCELLANEOUS — Ratings" herein)

In the opinion of Bond Counsel, under existing laws, regulations and judicial decisions, and assuming continued compliance by the Authority and the City with certain covenants in the Bond Resolution and the Lease, respectively, interest on the Series 2002 Bonds is exempt from present State of Georgia income taxation, is excluded from gross income for federal income tax purposes, and is not an item of tax preference for purposes of the federal individual and corporate alternative minimum tax; provided, however, with respect to corporations (as defined for federal income tax purposes), such interest is taken into account in determining adjusted current earnings for the purpose of computing the alternative minimum tax imposed on such corporations. See "LEGAL MATTERS — Tax Exemption."

$11,200,000
THOMASTON-UPSON COUNTY OFFICE BUILDING AUTHORITY (GEORGIA)
REVENUE BONDS, SERIES 2002

Dated: November 1, 2002   **Due: December 1, as shown below**

The Series 2002 Bonds are being issued by the Thomaston-Upson County Office Building Authority (Georgia) (the "Authority") for the purpose of (i) refunding an existing promissory note of the Authority in the outstanding principal amount of $6,728,559 (the "Note"), (ii) acquiring, constructing, installing and equipping certain components of the City of Thomaston's (the "City") combined water and sewerage and electric system (the "System"), and (iii) paying the costs of issuing the Series 2002 Bonds. See "APPLICATION OF FUNDS — Estimated Sources and Uses of Funds and — The Refunding."

The Authority and the City have heretofore entered into a Lease Contract, dated as of November 1, 2002 (the "Lease"), pursuant to which the City will pay to the Authority (the "Lease Payments") amounts sufficient to enable the Authority to pay the debt service on the Series 2002 Bonds and to levy an ad valorem tax on all property in the City subject to such tax in the event that the "Net Revenues" (hereinafter defined) are insufficient to pay debt service on the Series 2002 Bonds. The Series 2002 Bonds are special limited obligations of the Authority secured by and payable solely from a first lien pledge of the Lease Payments. The Series 2002 Bonds do not constitute a charge, lien or encumbrance, legal or equitable, on any other property of the Authority. See "THE SERIES 2002 BONDS — Security and Sources of Payment."

Payment of the principal of and interest on the Series 2002 Bonds when due will be guaranteed by a municipal bond insurance policy to be issued simultaneously with the delivery of the Series 2002 Bonds by MBIA Insurance Corporation. See "THE POLICY AND THE BOND INSURER" and APPENDIX F.

MBIA

Interest on the Series 2002 Bonds is payable semiannually on June 1 and December 1 of each year, commencing on June 1, 2003. All Series 2002 Bonds bear interest from November 1, 2002. See "INTRODUCTION — Description of the Series 2002 Bonds."

The Series 2002 Bonds are subject to redemption prior to maturity, as more fully described herein. See "THE SERIES 2002 BONDS."

MATURITIES, AMOUNTS, INTEREST RATES AND YIELDS

Maturity	Amount	Rate	Yield	Maturity	Amount	Rate	Yield
2003	$230,000	2.500%	1.600%	2013	$390,000	4.000%	3.820%*
2004	295,000	2.500	1.830	2014	405,000	4.000	4.020
2005	305,000	2.500	2.130	2015	420,000	4.100	4.170
2006	310,000	2.500	2.430	2016	440,000	4.200	4.300
2007	320,000	3.000	2.730	2017	455,000	4.300	4.400
2008	330,000	3.000	3.010	2018	475,000	4.400	4.500
2009	340,000	3.200	3.250	2019	495,000	4.500	4.600
2010	350,000	3.400	3.470	2020	520,000	4.600	4.700
2011	360,000	3.500	3.570	2021	545,000	4.625	4.770
2012	375,000	4.000	3.670	2022	570,000	4.700	4.850

$3,270,000 4.750% Term Bonds Due December 1, 2027 Priced to Yield 4.900%
(Plus accrued interest from November 1, 2002)

* Yield to the December 1, 2012 call at 100%.

The Series 2002 Bonds shall not be deemed to constitute a debt or general obligation of the State of Georgia or the City nor a pledge of the faith and credit of the State of Georgia or the City, nor shall the State of Georgia or the City be subject to any pecuniary liability thereon. The Authority has no taxing power.

THIS COVER PAGE CONTAINS CERTAIN INFORMATION FOR QUICK REFERENCE ONLY. IT IS NOT A SUMMARY OF THIS ISSUE. INVESTORS MUST READ THE ENTIRE OFFICIAL STATEMENT TO OBTAIN INFORMATION ESSENTIAL TO THE MAKING OF AN INFORMED INVESTMENT DECISION.

The Series 2002 Bonds are offered when, as and if issued and received by the Underwriter, subject to prior sale, to withdrawal or modification of the offer without notice, and subject to approval of legality by Smith Gambrell & Russell, LLP, Bond Counsel. Certain legal matters are subject to the approval of Adams, Barfield, Hankinson, Evans & Miller, LLP, Thomaston, Georgia, Counsel to the City and the Authority; and King & Spalding, Atlanta, Georgia, Underwriter's Counsel. The Series 2002 Bonds are expected to be delivered through The Depository Trust Company in New York, New York, on about November 6, 2002.

Salomon Smith Barney

October 15, 2002

want bonds from a particular state or bonds with certain quality grades or maturities. The better you are able to define the type of bond you want to purchase, the fewer unnecessary calls you will receive from brokers. The more firms you contact, the more likely you are to locate a new bond issue that interests you. Unless you are retired with nothing else to do, however, there is a limit to the amount of time and effort you may want to spend on such a task. The question of how many firms to contact depends in large part upon how quickly you want to make the purchase. If you are in no hurry, contacts with one or two large firms should prove adequate.

Corporate Issues

Corporations generally negotiate the terms of bond issues with investment banking firms with which the corporations have a continuing relationship. Businesses tend to establish long-term relationships with investment banking firms that keep them abreast of developments in the financial markets. An investment bank will assist in planning a new bond issue and, when the terms of the issue are complete, form a syndicate to distribute the bonds to investors. Corporations expect investment bankers to develop creative debt securities that will appeal to investors and reduce the cost of borrowing.

Like municipal bonds, corporate bonds are generally issued at a price at or near face value. Bonds are issued at face value by setting the bond coupons at levels that are competitive with outstanding bonds. For example, if the current interest rate on medium-quality corporate notes is 7.5 percent, the coupon rate on a new issue of medium-quality notes will be established at 7.5 percent. Rather than selling an issue of serial bonds with a large range of maturity dates, corporations generally sell bond issues with a single maturity, although the issuer may be required to redeem a certain number of bonds each year until maturity. Corporate bonds are likely to be callable and may be subject to a sinking fund requirement.

Corporate bonds are distributed to investors in the same manner as municipal bonds. An entire corporate bond issue will be purchased by the firm's investment banking company, which puts together a syndicate of underwriters and a selling group. The members of the syndicate become responsible for locating investors who will purchase the bonds. Members of the syndicate and the selling group earn a profit on the spread between the price they pay for the bonds and the price at which the bonds are sold to investors. All members of the syndicate and selling group are required to sell the bonds at the same price during the underwriting period. As with municipal bonds, no commission is charged to investors who purchase corporate bonds that are part of a new issue. Many corporate bond issues are privately placed with large institutional buyers; thus, they are not offered to individual investors.

To purchase corporate bonds that are part of a new issue, you will need to contact one or more brokerage firms that underwrite corporate bond issues. The more firms you alert to the fact that you are interested in purchasing corporate bonds, the quicker you are likely to learn about bonds that satisfy your investment needs. Before calling a broker you should make a list of the qualities you are seeking in a bond including credit quality, maturity length, industry preference, and yield expectations.

How Bonds Are Traded in the Secondary Market

Once issued, bonds are traded among dealers and investors in the secondary market. Without a secondary market, an investor who wanted to buy or sell bonds would be required to personally locate another investor who wanted to take the opposite side of the trade. Buyers would have to search for sellers, and sellers would have to search for buyers. Suppose 10 years ago you purchased $10,000 face amount of a new corporate bond issue with a 20-year maturity. Although you intended to hold the bonds for the full 20 years, you have recently encountered a financial emergency that causes you to need the cash you have invested in the bonds. Where do you turn? Without a secondary market you might have to advertise in a newspaper or contact friends who may have an interest in buying the bonds. Either way you are in a bind and will probably have to accept an unusually low price even if you are able to locate a potential buyer.

Fortunately for both issuers and investors, a secondary market provides an outlet for buyers and sellers of outstanding bonds. Billions of dollars worth of outstanding bonds are traded daily in this market. The existence of a secondary market benefits investors who wish to sell bonds at the same time that it significantly expands the variety of bonds that are made available to investors who would like to acquire these securities. The added liquidity of a secondary market also benefits issuers of bonds. How many investors would buy long-term bonds that were nearly impossible to sell prior to their scheduled maturities?

The Secondary Market for Bonds

Unlike common stocks of well-known companies that are listed and actively traded on organized securities exchanges, the vast majority of bonds, including U.S. Treasury securities, U.S. federal agency bonds, and municipal bonds, are traded in the over-the-counter (OTC) market. The OTC market comprises a large network of securities dealers who act as market makers by buying and selling bonds for their own accounts. Dealers in the over-the-counter market are connected with one another

> **Tip** Bond prices in the secondary market are sometimes negotiable. If a broker provides you with a quote on a bond you might save some money by asking for a better price. A better price means a lower price (higher yield for you) if you are buying and a higher price (lower yield for the buyer) if you are selling. You are more likely to obtain a better price when you are buying or selling a relatively large amount of bonds.

and with other financial institutions through sophisticated communications equipment that eliminates the need for a formal trading floor.

Not all bonds are traded exclusively in the over-the-counter market. The New York Stock Exchange lists several thousand corporate bond issues, and the American Stock Exchange lists approximately five hundred corporate bonds. A limited number of corporate bonds are also traded on the regional exchanges. Despite the large number of bonds that are listed for trading on the exchanges, the trading volume of these bonds is quite small compared to over-the-counter trading of corporate bonds. Average daily corporate bond volume on the organized exchanges normally amounts to less than 1 percent of the average daily volume of corporate bond trading in the over-the-counter market. Bonds listed on the organized exchanges are generally bought and sold in modest amounts by individual investors rather than by institutional investors that require the liquidity of the over-the-counter market for their large trades. Many listed bond issues do not trade for days or weeks at a time.

Daily trading of U.S. Treasury securities far surpasses secondary trading of corporate bonds. A relatively small number of primary dealers serve as the major market makers who provide bids and ask quotations for all Treasury securities. The dealers also work closely with the Federal Reserve in supplying information about the financial markets and assisting the Fed with its own buying and selling of Treasury securities.

The secondary market for municipal bonds consists of many dealers around the country that specialize in trading tax-exempt bonds. Each dealer holds a variety of bonds that have been acquired from investors or from other dealers. Although a dealer is free to trade whatever municipal bonds become available, most dealers concentrate on maintaining bond inventories that are most likely to appeal to their own customers. For example, a municipal bond dealer in St. Louis is likely to maintain a relatively large inventory on bonds issued in Missouri and Illinois. Likewise, a dealer in San Francisco who primarily serves California clients will buy and sell mostly California bonds.

The secondary market in municipal bonds is very fragmented, mainly because so many different municipal bond issues trade in the secondary market. Many municipal issues are relatively small in size, making it likely that bonds from these issues are infrequently traded in the secondary market. Also, large blocks of some issues end up in the portfolios of institutions that intend to hold the bonds until redemption. At any given time, only a small number of most bond issues are available for trading in the secondary market.

Buying Bonds in the Secondary Market

Institutional investors that engage in very large trades of corporate, municipal, and U.S. government securities dominate the secondary bond market. Trades of $5,000 and $10,000 by individual investors are the exception rather than the rule in the secondary market. Because institutional investors dominate the secondary market in bonds, individual investors generally pay a higher price to buy a particular bond and receive a lower price to sell a particular bond compared to the prices paid and received by institutional investors. The price differences can sometimes be relatively large.

Excluding Treasury securities, a broker is most likely to show you bonds that are being held in the firm's inventory. The bond departments of most large broker-dealers maintain a continuous inventory of bonds that they offer for resale to clients and to other dealers. Some of the inventory has been purchased from the firm's customers and other bonds have been acquired from competing dealers. The more firms you contact, the greater the variety of bonds you will be offered. You are also likely to discover that the prices offered on similar bonds can be different at different firms.

When you contact a broker to search for a bond to purchase, the broker will first ask for a general description of the type of bond you would like to buy, including such characteristics as maturity length, credit quality, type of issue (e.g., corporate, U.S. Treasury, municipal), if it matters whether the bond is priced at a premium or a discount, and so forth. After noting your preferences the broker will search the firm's inventory for bonds that come closest to meeting your requirements. If the firm is not currently holding bonds that meet your specifications and you are willing to wait several days or weeks before making an investment, you can request that the broker continue searching for suitable bonds.

If you are interested in owning bonds that can be bought and sold in relatively small amounts, you might want to consider sticking with corporate bonds listed for trading on one of the exchanges. Listed bonds frequently trade in small volume and there is no penalty for buying and selling several bonds at a time. Another advantage to owning listed bonds is you are able to check the daily newspaper quotations to determine if your bond traded the previous day and, if so, at what price. One word of caution: Consider entering a limit order that specifies the highest price you will pay when you are buying bonds and the lowest price you will accept when you are selling bonds. Bonds that trade in small volume are subject to sudden price changes, which can result in executions at prices substantially different from those you expect. Specifying a price will protect you from an unpleasant surprise.

Individual investors should generally follow a policy of buying bonds with the idea of holding the securities until maturity or the expected call dates. Having a bond redeemed generally involves no price concession or brokerage fee. Buying a bond with the intention of holding it to maturity means that you should be very selective about the maturity lengths of the bonds you purchase. Rather than merely buy a long-term bond with any maturity between 20 and 30 years, you should identify as closely as possible when you will need the principal and then purchase a bond with an appropriate maturity.

In truth, most individuals with modest amounts to invest are probably better off buying shares of investment companies or unit trusts that invest in bonds rather than buying individual bond issues. Investment companies are able to negotiate better prices, obtain lower commissions, and achieve better diversification than most individual investors. The costs imposed by investment companies can be reduced if you spend time shopping among the great number of funds that specialize in bonds. Investment companies generally specialize in government bonds, corporate bonds, municipal bonds, long-term government bonds, and so forth. No matter what you need, you will almost surely find one or more bond funds that have established goals that are compatible with your own goals. Chapter 6 presents a more complete discussion of bond funds and trusts.

6 Ready-Made Bond Portfolios: Investment Companies and Trusts

I ndividual investors seeking current income can benefit from the diversification, liquidity, and professional management offered by investment companies and unit investment trusts. Both investment companies and unit trusts pool investors' funds in a portfolio of financial assets including bonds. Your own financial resources and goals are important in determining which of these investments best suits your own needs. Careful selection will permit you to minimize the fees you will be required to pay to own investment companies and trusts.

Investment companies and unit investment trusts (UITs) pool investors' money to purchase financial assets including stocks, bonds, and money market instruments. The assets are selected and managed by professional investment managers who presumably possess the knowledge and experience to make informed investment decisions. Some investment companies and UITs invest only in common stocks while other companies invest only in bonds or in a combination of stocks and bonds. Although investment companies and unit investment trusts offer the same basic product—a portfolio of professionally selected financial assets—the two organizations differ with respect to business structure, sales and management fees, and investment philosophies. Substantial differences also exist among investment companies and among unit investment trusts, especially with regard to the investments that are held in the firms' portfolios.

An investment company is an ongoing firm that owns an actively managed portfolio of financial assets. The firm employs professional investment managers who assemble a portfolio of securities that is continually monitored, evaluated, and altered as the managers attempt to improve the shareholders' returns. Open-end investment companies, popularly known as *mutual*

Figure 10 ■ **Number of Bond Funds, 1985–2001**

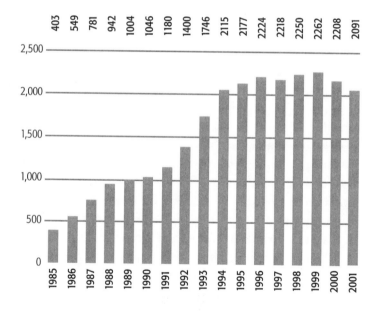

funds, comprise the majority of investment companies. A mutual fund has an unusual corporate structure that allows the continuous creation and liquidation of its own shares. Closed-end investment companies are less popular among investors who are interested in equities but very popular among individuals who prefer bond investments. Closed-end funds are organized in a manner identical to typical corporations; the company issues a limited number of ownership shares that subsequently trade in the secondary market. Figure 10 illustrates the increased number of investment companies devoted to bond portfolios. The third alternative, investment trusts, are created with unmanaged portfolios and limited lives. A trust is formed with an initial portfolio of securities that remains unchanged except when bonds are redeemed and principal is returned to the trust. Funds from bond redemptions, along with interest and dividends, are paid to the trust's owners. A unit trust is dissolved when most of the bonds in its portfolio have been redeemed.

Mutual Funds

Mutual funds enjoy the greatest popularity among the three types of investment organizations discussed in this chapter. This type of investment company is especially popular among investors who wish to own a portfolio of common stocks. Mutual fund sponsors spend enormous sums of money on advertising in an attempt to convince investors that they offer a convenient and superior method for investing in stocks and bonds. By the end of 2003 more than $7 billion in financial assets were held by 8,231 mutual funds.

> **Tip** Mutual funds are permitted to levy a variety of fees that will reduce the return you earn as a shareholder. Fees are especially important for individuals who invest in bond funds because of the relatively modest yield these funds provide. Always check a mutual fund's fee schedule before you purchase shares in the fund.

How Mutual Funds Are Organized

Mutual funds issue shares of ownership and utilize the proceeds to acquire financial assets including stocks and bonds. Individuals who purchase shares of a mutual fund become part owners of the fund's portfolio. Some mutual funds (called *stock*, or *equity funds*) invest only in common stocks, while other mutual funds (*bond funds*) specialize in bond investments. Still other funds (*balanced funds*) hold portfolios that are a combination of both stocks and bonds. Most mutual funds not only specialize in either stocks or bonds, but hold a portfolio that is concentrated in a particular category of stocks or bonds. For example, a bond fund might attempt to provide its owners with high levels of current income by investing mostly in high-risk, high-yielding bonds. Figure 11 (pp. 100–101) provides an overview of the various categories of mutual funds that are available to investors.

Mutual funds continually offer for sale new shares of their own stock at the same time they stand ready to redeem their outstanding shares. A fund will occasionally grow very rapidly or become so large that the sponsors decide to suspend the sale of new shares (although not the redemption of outstanding shares). For example, a firm's sponsor may feel that managing a very large portfolio hinders investment results and so decide to close the fund to new investors. In theory no limit exists to the number of shares a mutual fund can issue, and some funds hold portfolios of enormous size.

Mutual funds are able to redeem their own shares on demand because the assets they hold are relatively easy to convert into cash. Also, mutual funds enjoy continuous inflows of cash from the sale of new shares. Funds received from the sale of new shares can be utilized to pay for at least a portion of the shares being redeemed. Ordinary companies that have substantial amounts of fixed assets such as buildings and equipment cannot continually buy and sell their shares as do mutual funds. For example, an industrial company such as ExxonMobil cannot be expected to sell pieces of its drilling rigs, office buildings, or oil reserves whenever some of the firm's stockholders decide they would like to cash in their shares. Mutual funds hold liquid financial assets that tend to be actively traded in secondary markets. The liquidity of their assets permits the funds to easily liquidate a portion of their stock and bond portfolios whenever the need arises.

The market value of assets held in a mutual fund portfolio continually changes as the mutual fund issues new shares and redeems outstanding shares. The portfolio also changes in value as the values of the investment assets it owns experience price changes. A mutual fund that experiences several consecutive periods of favorable investment results will typically attract a large inflow of money from investors who wish to invest in the fund. The inflow of money means that the fund's manager must find stocks and/or bonds in which to invest this money. During periods of poor performance, shareholder redemptions are likely to exceed the sale of new shares, causing a mutual fund to contract in size as a portion of the fund's securities are sold in order to pay for the redeemed shares. A mutual fund is in some ways similar to a bathtub in which water is always flowing into the tub at the same time the drain is always open. Water flowing from the spigot represents new money that is entering the fund and water flowing down the drain represents money being paid to the fund's shareholders who are submitting their shares for redemption. Water remaining in the bathtub representing assets of the fund is constantly expanding and contracting as the two flows change.

Mutual fund shares are not ordinarily listed for trading on the national or regional exchanges, and they are not traded in the

---

Figure 11 ■ Categories of Bond Funds

Types of Corporate Bond Funds

Corporate Bond Fund: General—At least two-thirds of the portfolio invested in U.S. corporate bonds with no restriction on average maturity length.

Corporate Bond Fund: Intermediate-Term—At least two-thirds of the portfolio invested in U.S. corporate bonds with an average maturity of five to ten years.

Corporate Bond Fund: Short-Term—At least two-thirds of the portfolio invested in U.S. corporate bonds with an average maturity of one to five years.

High-Yield Corporate Bond Fund—At least two-thirds of the portfolio invested in U.S. corporate bonds rated Baa or lower by Moody's and BBB or lower by Standard and Poor's bond rating services.

Types of World Bond Funds

Global Bond Fund: General—At least three-quarters of the portfolio invested in foreign debt securities with no restriction on average maturity length.

Global Bond Fund: Short-Term—At least three-quarters of the portfolio invested in foreign debt securities with an average maturity of one to five years.

Other World Bond Funds—At least two-thirds of the portfolio invested in a particular segment of foreign debt securities such as emerging markets or a particular country or region.

over-the-counter market. These shares don't need to be listed because mutual fund shareholders can liquidate their investment by submitting shares directly to the sponsors or to agents of the sponsors. By having the mutual fund redeem their stock, shareholders are not required to pay a commission to a broker in order to locate another investor that will purchase the shares.

Types of Government Bond Funds

Government Bond Fund: General—At least two-thirds of the portfolio invested in U.S. government securities with no restriction on average maturity length.

Government Bond Fund: Intermediate-Term—At least two-thirds of the portfolio invested in U.S. government securities with an average maturity of five to ten years.

Government Bond Fund: Short-Term—At least two-thirds of the portfolio invested in U.S. government securities with an average maturity of one to five years.

Mortgage-Backed Fund—At least two-thirds of the portfolio invested in mortgaged-backed securities.

Strategic Income Fund—A portfolio with a combination of U.S. debt securities.

Types of Municipal Bond Funds

State Municipal Bond Fund: General—Majority of the portfolio invested in municipal bonds issued within a particular state. The average maturity is greater than five years.

State Municipal Bond Fund: Short-Term—A portfolio of municipal bonds issued within a particular state. The average maturity is one to five years.

National Municipal Bond Fund: General—Majority of the portfolio invested in municipal bonds with an average maturity of over five years.

National Municipal Bond Fund: Short-Term—Majority of the portfolio invested in municipal bonds with an average maturity of one to five years.

> **Tip**
>
> Buying shares of a mutual fund directly from the fund rather than through a broker can help you to avoid a sales charge. The sales charge is designed to compensate the salesperson, not the portfolio manager, so there is no reason to believe that lack of a sales charge will result in a mutual fund turning in an inferior investment performance.

Federal regulations require that virtually all realized capital gains, dividends, and interest received by a mutual fund be passed through to the fund's shareholders who assume any tax obligation. Essentially, a mutual fund is a conduit that collects capital gains, dividends, and interest that it pays to the fund's owners. The greater the gains in the portfolio that are realized through asset sales, the larger the capital gains distributions to shareholders. Likewise, larger dividend distributions are made by mutual funds that receive more dividends and interest from the assets they hold. A mutual fund that invests in bonds generally receives substantially more current income and pays more dividends to its to stockholders compared to a mutual fund that invests in stocks. On the downside, bond funds generally offer substantially less opportunity than stock funds for investors to enjoy capital gains distributions or large increases in the market value of their shares.

Birth of the Kudzu Fund

To better explain how a mutual fund functions, it may be helpful to organize our own hypothetical fund. Suppose that you and nine of your investment buddies decide to pool your funds and start an investment company that you name the Kudzu Fund. The name is selected for the rapid growth experienced by this plant that you hope translates to the fund's value. The initial task of your group is to determine the investment goal or goals to be pursued by the fund. Are you and your fellow owners interested in maximizing current income or are you seeking investments that offer the possibility for large gains in market value? The goals will establish a standard for the types of securities the fund should acquire and hold. Because you purchased this book to learn about bonds, suppose we assume you and the other owners decide on a goal of maximum current income and restrict the fund's investments to corporate bonds. You could have chosen the safety of U.S. government bonds or the growth potential of stocks, of course, but corporate bonds should result in higher annual dividend distributions for shareholders. The members of your investment group decide to start the fund with $50,000 of investment capital. The initial share price of the fund could be established at any level, but it is decided to issue shares at a price of $10 each. Thus, issuing 5,000 shares will allow the fund to commence operations with the desired $50,000.

The fund chooses to invest in $10,000 face amount of each of three corporate bond issues and $15,000 in a fourth issue. Two of the purchases are made at par value of $1,000 per bond and the other two issues are purchased at discounted prices of $900 and $800 per bond, respectively. The $9,000 not used to purchase bonds is placed in a money market fund and the mutual fund's beginning portfolio will be as shown in Figure 12.

The four bond issues owned by the Kudzu Fund will produce total annual interest income of $2,750 ($700 from Rushville bonds, $600 from KLS bonds, $700 from Gnat bonds, and $750 from Blazer bonds) that will be supplemented by nominal income from the money market fund. If the money-market fund deposit earns an annual return of 4 percent, $360 in additional interest income (4 percent of $9,000) will cause the fund

Figure 12 ■ Portfolio of Kudzu Fund

Issue	Number of Bonds	Face Value	Price	Market Value
Rushville Corp 7% of 15	10	$10,000	$1,000	$10,000
KLS Corp 6% of 16	10	10,000	1,000	10,000
Gnat Corp 7% of 12	10	10,000	900	9,000
Blazer, Inc 5% of 14	15	15,000	800	12,000
Total bonds				$41,000
Money market fund				9,000
Total fund assets				$50,000
Shares of Kudzu Fund outstanding				5,000
Net asset value (total assets/shares outstanding)				$10

to pay total first year dividends of $3,110, or 62.2¢ for each of the 5,000 shares. If you invested $5,000 and purchased 500 shares of the fund's stock on the initial issue date, you will receive dividends of $311 during the fund's first year of operation. Buying shares of a mutual fund causes you to hitch your financial wagon to the fund's portfolio and the investing expertise of the fund's portfolio manager.

Establishing a Mutual Fund's Share Value

Mutual fund shares are priced according to the share's *net asset value* (NAV). This is the financial statistic that most interests a mutual fund shareholder because it establishes the price at which the fund issues new shares and the price the fund pays for redeemed shares. NAV doesn't consider sales or redemption fees that a fund may levy. Net asset value is the price published on Internet sites and in the financial sections of most daily newspapers. The NAV of each outstanding share is equal to the total value of a fund's assets (less any debts) divided by the number of the fund's outstanding shares. With no debts, the Kudzu Fund has an initial net asset value of $50,000/5,000 shares, or $10, which is the price you and the other investors paid for the shares. The net asset value of a fund fluctuates with changes in the market values of securities held in the fund's portfolio. An increase in the market values of bonds in the fund's portfolio will cause an increase in the fund's net asset value. Conversely, a general decline in bond values will cause a decline in a bond fund's NAV. Any distributions of capital from the fund to shareholders will cause a reduction in the fund's assets and result in a decline in the fund's net asset value.

Now suppose we move forward one year in the life of the Kudzu Fund. You and the other investors have been satisfied with the bonds that were initially acquired and no changes have been made in the fund's portfolio. Market interest rates declined slightly during the year, causing the market values of bonds in the portfolio to increase from $41,000 to $44,800. Combined with $9,000 in money market fund balances that remain unaffected by interest rate changes, the total portfolio of the fund now amounts to $53,800, an increase of $3,800 compared to the original portfolio. No new shares have been issued and none of the initial shares have been redeemed so the net asset value for each of the fund's shares has increased to $53,800/5,000, or $10.76. You and the other owners have benefited both from the dividends you received and from the increased value of each of the shares you hold. The 62.2-cent dividend combined with the 76-cent gain in share value produced an overall return of $1.382/$10.00, or 13.82 percent for the year.

Altering the composition of a mutual fund's portfolio (that is, selling some securities and replacing them with different securities) does not affect the fund's net asset value at the time the change occurs. If a fund sells $20,000 of one bond issue and uses the proceeds to acquire $20,000 of a different bond issue, the total value of the fund's portfolio and the net asset value of the fund's shares remains unchanged. Likewise, the total assets of a mutual fund remain unchanged if the fund uses money being held in a money market fund to pay for the purchase of additional bonds. Over a period of weeks or months, the new securities may prove to be superior investments compared to the securities being replaced. Altering a portfolio to include securities that provide superior appreciation will eventually result in a higher NAV than if the portfolio had remained unchanged. Mutual fund portfolio managers are paid to make these decisions.

Distributions to Mutual Fund Shareholders

A mutual fund is required to distribute to its shareholders the dividends and interest that are received from securities held in the fund's portfolio. In addition, gains realized from the sale of securities must be distributed to shareholders. For example, if a fund pays $20,000 for bonds that are later sold for $24,000, the $4,000 gain that is realized from the sale must be passed through as a capital gains distribution to the fund's shareholders. Dividends, interest, and realized capital gains that are passed through to mutual fund shareholders are taxable to the shareholders but not to the mutual fund. In general, capital gains distributions are of secondary importance to bond fund investors who are primarily interested in the current income from interest income earned by the funds and passed through to shareholders.

The Distribution of Mutual Fund Shares

Many mutual fund sponsors distribute their shares directly to investors. Individuals purchase shares of these mutual funds by sending checks or wiring funds to the sponsors. Share redemptions are also made directly through the sponsors. Mutual funds that sell directly do not require salespeople, although advertising is utilized in order to attract investors. The best advertising is free and simply consists of superior investment performance that will be widely reported to the public.

Other mutual funds choose to distribute their shares through salespeople including brokers, insurance agents, and financial planners. Virtually all brokerage firms offer mutual funds to their customers. Large brokerage firms even distribute some of their own in-house mutual funds as well as mutual funds sponsored by outside firms.

To purchase mutual fund shares directly from the sponsor you must be willing to select on your own which particular fund to buy. This means you must choose the sponsor from which to buy as well as the type of fund to own (long-term corporate bonds, intermediate-maturity municipal bonds, high-yield bonds, and so forth). Mutual fund sponsors that sell directly to investors will provide plenty of written material, and you can talk with the sponsor's salespeople. You will also find an enormous amount of information on mutual fund sponsor websites. Still, with direct sellers you are pretty much on your own to select a fund that is appropriate to meet the investment goals you deem important.

If you choose to purchase mutual fund shares from a sponsor that distributes its funds through commissioned salespeople, you may be able to obtain worthwhile investment advice, especially if the salesperson you contact represents many different funds from several different sponsors. A salesperson with access to many different products is more likely to represent a fund that fits your investment needs. Still, you must keep in the back of your mind that the salesperson may try to steer you toward funds that pay the largest sales commission to the salesperson.

Mutual Fund Fees

Mutual funds levy a variety of charges. These firms are in the business to make money for the shareholders, of course, but they are also interested in making money for their managers and sponsors. Different funds levy different and varying amounts of charges. These charges cause you to earn a lower return on your investment, so it is important that you understand fully what charges are being applied and how the charges are calculated. Investigate charges imposed by a fund before, not after, you invest.

Mutual funds that sell their shares through commissioned salespeople normally levy a sales charge, or *load*, that pays the salespeople for their time and effort. The charge is added on top of a fund's net asset value and results in an investor paying more to purchase shares than if no sales charge is imposed. Sales charges vary among funds, but most bond funds with a load charge approximately 3 to 4 percent of the amount invested. Funds that levy a sales charge are called *load funds*. Funds that levy a relatively small sales charge are called *low-load funds*. Funds that do not charge a sales fee are called *no-load funds*.

Some mutual funds levy a fee at the time shares are redeemed rather than when shares are purchased. For example, you may purchase shares of a particular fund at net asset value but be required to pay a fee of 3 to 4 percent of net asset value when shares are submitted for redemption. Some mutual funds reduce redemption fees when shares have been held a prescribed number of years. For example, a mutual fund might levy a 6-percent fee for redeemed shares that have been held a year or less, 5-percent for shares held one to two years, and so forth. This type of schedule generally allows you to escape a redemption fee altogether if shares have been held a specified number of years.

Mutual funds that distribute their shares directly to investors do not employ the services of commissioned salespeople and generally do not levy a sales fee. These no-load funds sell their shares at net asset value and all of an investor's money is used to purchase shares of the fund. No-load funds reduce their distribution expenses by eliminating payments to salespeople. Mutual funds have other marketing expenses besides paying people to sell their shares, so all funds have at least some distribution expenses they must cover.

An increasing number of mutual funds levy a relatively small annual distribution and marketing expense called a *12b–1 fee* that is periodically charged against a fund's assets. Because this is an annual charge, the longer you own a mutual fund with a 12b–1 fee, the greater the accumulated cost to you. Numerous mutual funds charge both a sales or redemption fee *and* a 12b–1 fee. A mutual fund's fee income from 12b–1 charges is utilized to attract additional investors rather than to improve the investment performance of the fund's portfolio. Critics claim that 12b–1 fees are nothing other than hidden sales charges.

All mutual funds incur operating expenses, including rent, utilities, postage, portfolio management fees, and so forth. The funds cover these expenses by levying an annual fee against assets that ranges from as low as one-fifth of one percent of assets to 1.5 or 2 percent of assets. In general, the ratio of expenses to assets is lower for bond funds than for stock funds. Fees to cover operating expenses result in a direct reduction in the income that would otherwise be distributed to a mutual fund's shareholders.

Many mutual funds charge no sales fee, no redemption fee, and no 12b–1 fee. You should closely investigate a mutual fund's fee structure before committing your money to acquiring its shares. If you feel that you are knowledgeable enough to select an appropriate mutual fund on your own, there may be little reason to incur the added expense of dealing with a salesperson. On the other hand, a sales fee may be a worthwhile expenditure if you are a novice investor who requires assistance in selecting a mutual fund. One other thing to keep in mind: Various studies indicate that mutual funds without a sales fee tend to levy slightly higher annual charges.

Closed-End Investment Companies

Closed-end investment companies are sometimes called *publicly-traded investment companies* or *closed-end funds* because they issue a fixed number of shares that are traded in the secondary market. Closed-end equity funds have never achieved the prominence of their mutual fund relatives, but closed-end funds that specialize in bond portfolios are very popular. Mutual funds spend huge sums of money to market their shares to investors. A greater number of shares results in more assets under management and higher fee income for the managers. A closed-end fund has a fixed number of shares, so the firm's management has little interest in attracting additional investors once the fund's shares have been issued.

Certain closed-end bond funds use leverage (debt) to increase the amount of money invested in bonds. These firms, called *leveraged closed-end bond funds*, take out short-term loans and utilize the proceeds to purchase additional bonds for the fund's portfolio. During periods of steady interest rates, these leveraged funds can earn additional interest income on the differential between long-term interest rates and short-term interest rates. During periods of declining interest rates, a leveraged fund can earn additional income on portfolio gains resulting from rising bond values. During periods of rising interest rates, leveraged bond funds run into trouble as the value of their portfolios declines at the same time they must pay higher interest charges on borrowed money. Leveraged bond funds offer a greater potential for profit at the expense of greater risk of loss for shareholders.

Shares of closed-end investment companies are bought and sold through brokerage companies. The brokerage commissions are the same as if you purchased shares of General Motors or Goodyear. The brokerage firm, not the investment company, establishes the commission you must pay. It is worthwhile to shop among brokerage companies when purchasing shares of a closed-end fund because brokerage commissions vary significantly from firm to firm. You will also be required to pay a brokerage fee when the shares are sold. On the positive side, closed-end funds do not levy their own sales and redemption fees.

Management of a Closed-End Investment Company

A closed-end fund offers the same basic product as a mutual fund—a relatively large and diversified or specialized portfolio of a particular type of security (for example, common stocks, government bonds, municipal bonds, corporate bonds, and so forth) that is supervised by professional investment managers. Income earned by a closed-end bond fund is paid to the fund's stockholders in monthly or quarterly dividend payments. The more interest income a fund earns from the bonds it holds, the larger the dividends that will be paid to the fund's shareholders.

Investment advisers are paid to actively manage the bond

portfolios of closed-end investment companies. The managers monitor the company's portfolio for securities they feel are overpriced, and at the same time search for undervalued bonds to substitute for debt securities the fund already owns. Closed-end investment companies do not have additional cash flowing in from the sale of new shares, so the managers trade securities in the firm's portfolio rather than add securities to the portfolio. Likewise, the managers of closed-end funds do not need to be concerned about share redemptions that would likely force them to sell bonds in order to come up with cash to pay for the redeemed shares.

The annual charges that cover operating expenses and pay the portfolio managers cause a reduction in a fund's profits and a resulting decline in shareholder distributions. If an investment company annually incurs operating expenses of $500,000, there is $500,000 less money available to distribute to the fund's shareholders. Of course, the stockholders hope that the fund's portfolio managers will make good investment decisions that allow the fund to cover its expenses and still earn higher returns than shareholders could earn on alternative investments.

The Pricing of Closed-End Funds

The shares of a closed-end investment company are priced at whatever value investors in the secondary market decide the shares are worth. A closed-end fund does not redeem its own shares at net asset value, so stockholders who wish to liquidate their shares must accept the going price being paid at the time the transaction occurs. Shares of a closed-end investment company may sell either above (at a premium) or below (at a discount) net asset value.

The net asset value of a closed-end fund is calculated in the same manner as a mutual fund; that is, the current value of the fund's portfolio less any debt is divided by the number of out-standing shares. An investment company with a $40 million bond portfolio, no debt, and 5 million outstanding shares has a net asset value of $40 million/5 million shares, or $8.00 per share. Increases in the fund's portfolio value will cause the investment company's net asset value to increase by a propor-tional amount. Likewise, a decline in the value of bonds held in the fund's portfolio will cause a decline in net asset value.

Uncertainty regarding whether a closed-end fund's shares will trade above or below net asset value at the time you are ready to sell your stock causes greater uncertainty about the price you will receive. You not only wonder what will happen to net asset value, but whether the shares will trade at a premium or discount to net asset value. You may receive a lower price than you paid for the stock even though the fund's net asset value increased during your holding period. Even if you pur-chase closed-end fund shares at a discount from net asset value, you may discover that the discount has increased by the time you are ready to sell the shares.

Unit Investment Trusts

Unit investment trusts (UITs), also called *unit trusts*, offer a third alternative for acquiring a portfolio of securities. UITs that hold bond portfolios, especially tax-exempt bond portfolios, are quite popular among investors who seek current income. The unique organizational structure of unit trusts allows investors who own units of a trust (that is, pieces of ownership similar to shares of stock) to determine exactly how much principal will eventually be returned even though they are unsure exactly when the principal will be returned.

The Organization of Unit Investment Trusts

An investment trust holds a portfolio of securities that remains essentially unchanged throughout the trust's finite life. In the case of a trust that concentrates on bonds, the life is limited by the maturities of bonds in the portfolio. Whereas the life of a mutual fund and closed-end investment company goes on indefinitely as money received from bond sales or redemptions is reinvested in other bonds, a unit trust doesn't reinvest the funds it receives in additional bonds. Rather, the trust passes through to the trust's owners all of the payments that are received from bond redemptions. Like investment companies, the trust collects interest from the bonds that it owns and forwards this interest to the trust's owners. In addition, the trust passes through to the owners any principal payments that are received from redemptions.

The sponsor of a unit trust assembles the bonds that are to be included in the trust—typically ten to twelve different issues—and then issues a fixed number of units, or shares of ownership, to investors. The price at which the units are sold is determined by the value of the bonds in the portfolio and the number of units the trust issues. For example, the sponsor of a unit investment trust may acquire $100,000 each of ten different bond issues, resulting in a total portfolio value of $1 million. The sponsors may decide to issue 1,000 units of ownership with an issue price of $1,000 per unit.

Tip Unit trusts are most appropriate for investors who anticipate a long holding period. The fees for unit trusts are generally levied on the front end when the trust units are purchased. This one-time fee reduces an investor's return but is less important when the trust units are to be held for many years.

As a trust ages and bonds held in the portfolio are redeemed, the trust becomes smaller in size and its unit values decline proportionately. For example, fifteen years after the above-noted trust is formed with $1 million of bonds, the trust's portfolio may only contain $600,000 of the original bonds, the remainder having been redeemed by issuers. As bonds in a trust's portfolio are redeemed and principal is returned to the trust's owners, interest received by the trust will decline and reduced payments will be made to unit holders. Eventually, most of a trust's bonds will have been redeemed and the remaining bonds will be liquidated. At this point the life of the unit investment trust has come to an end.

The Cost of Investing in Unit Investment Trusts

Sponsors of a unit trust select bonds for the trust's portfolio and market ownership units to investors who are interested in earning current income. A unit trust with a fixed portfolio of bonds has no need for portfolio managers once the initial portfolio has been assembled. Without a need to supervise the portfolio, owners will not be hit with a substantial management fee similar to that charged by both mutual funds and closed-end investment companies. The lack of a management fee increases the annual return by $1/4$ percent to $1/2$ percent compared to the return from owning shares of an investment company that

> **Tip** A mutual fund sales fee is particularly important if you expect to have a relatively short holding period. The annual operating expense, rather than a sales fee, is more important if you are likely to have a long holding period. The best choice, of course, is a fund with no sales charge and a relatively small annual operating expense.

specializes in bonds.

Investment trust sponsors typically charge a sales fee that ranges from 2 to 5 percent of the money invested. The sales charge is added to the price of a unit. Purchase ten trust units at a price of $1,000 per unit and you will pay $10,000 plus the sponsor's sales charge. A sales fee of 3 percent would result in you being assessed an additional $300. Sponsors sometimes reduce the percentage sales fee for individuals who invest large sums of money. For example, a sponsor that normally charges a 4-percent sales fee may charge only 3 percent when more than $25,000 is invested.

The Value of a Unit

The value of an investment trust's units is determined by the current values of bonds held in the trust's portfolio divided by the outstanding units of ownership. If market rates of interest decline following distribution of a trust, the market values of bonds held in the trust's portfolio will increase. The amount of the increase depends upon the degree that interest rates decline and the maturities of the bonds that are owned. Longer maturities will result in larger bond price changes. If market rates of interest increase following a trust's distribution, the market values of bonds held in the trust's portfolio will decline. Again, the extent of the decline will depend on how much interest rates increase and the maturity lengths of bonds held by the trust.

Fluctuations in the value of a trust's units would not be particularly important if no outlet existed in which to sell units of trust ownership. If you are unable to resell units but know that all of your principal will eventually be returned, changes in the values of the trust's bonds may not be a concern. On the other hand, if there is a possibility you may need to sell your investment prior to the trust's eventual liquidation, you are likely to be very interested in the market values of bonds that are held in the trust's portfolio.

Most sponsors of unit investment trusts create a secondary market for the trusts they bring to market. Although an investor cannot have units of ownership redeemed in the manner of mutual fund shareholders, most sponsors will agree to buy back trust units that will then be offered for resale. Owners of trust units receive the bid prices (that is, the prices at which bonds could be sold) of bonds held in the trust's portfolio. Sponsors charge an additional sales fee for units that are sold in the secondary market.

Comparing Ready-Made Bond Portfolios

Each of the three investment vehicles discussed in this chapter offers a bond portfolio of varying diversification for a relatively small investment. The portfolios are frequently concentrated in a particular bond segment. Specialized portfolios include long-term bonds, intermediate-term bonds, municipal bonds, municipal bonds issued within a particular state, U.S. government bonds, and so forth. Where there is an investment need there is an investment company to sop up investors' money. Regardless of whether you choose a mutual fund, a closed-end investment company, or a unit investment trust, you must decide whether you want a specialized bond portfolio and, if so, what type.

Unit investment trusts are a good choice for investors who plan a relatively long holding period. The single initial sales fee and minimal operating expenses benefit long-term investors. The lack of an annual fee is important when you intend to hold the investment for many years. Unit trusts are particularly popular among investors who are interested in earning tax-exempt interest income but who are unable to come up with the substantial sum of money necessary to assemble a portfolio of municipal bonds that are issued in minimum denominations of $5,000.

Mutual fund shares offer excellent liquidity because they can be redeemed at any time through the sponsor. Equally important, many mutual funds levy neither a sales nor redemption fee. Mutual fund liquidity makes no-load funds a good choice if you plan a relatively short holding period. For example, if you are expecting interest rates to fall during the next six months, you may want to invest in a no-load mutual fund that holds a portfolio of long-term government bonds. You will be able to sell your shares at a profit if your forecast proves accurate.

The shares of closed-end investment companies frequently sell in the secondary market at a discount from net asset value. Thus, investing in one of these funds may offer an opportunity to buy into a bond portfolio at below the market value of the portfolio. Buying shares at a discount to net asset value should allow you to earn a higher current return than is available on comparable mutual funds. Keep in mind that the share price of a closed-end investment company fluctuates with respect to the firm's NAV, creating more uncertainty regarding the price you will receive when the shares are sold.

> **Tip**
> Mutual funds and closed-end investment companies are particularly attractive when you wish to invest in foreign bonds. Bonds issued in foreign countries and denominated in a foreign currency are generally more difficult to value and purchase compared to bonds traded in the United States. Thus, selecting these bonds is better left to the experts employed by investment companies.

7 The Risks of Investing in Bonds

Although bonds are generally considered safer investments than stocks, even high-quality debt securities subject investors to important risks that can produce unpleasant surprises. Bonds are less risky than stocks in some respects, but more risky than stocks in other respects. When considering an investment in bonds, you should be concerned about inflation, future interest rate changes, early redemptions, the current and future financial strength of the issuer, and the ease with which the bonds can be sold. Most risks can be reduced by carefully selecting bonds that meet your needs. Diversification is one important and painless method for reducing risk.

Any debt security will subject its owner to some degree of risk. Even short-term U.S. Treasury bills, generally considered to be among the safest of all investments, will cause investors concern about the rate of return they will be able to earn on reinvested proceeds. At the opposite end of the risk spectrum are junk bonds, debt securities of such great risk that they have brought financial ruin to investors who owned them and the organizations that issued them.

An Overview of Risk

Finance professionals view investment risk as the uncertainty of the return that will be earned from holding a particular asset or portfolio of assets. The more certain you are that an investment's expected return will be its actual return, the lower the risk of owning that investment. Savings accounts, certificates of deposit, and U.S. Treasury bills provide a very certain return and subject investors to relatively little risk. On the other hand, investments such as gold, collectible coins and stamps, and most common stock issues have very volatile market values and unpredictable returns, which make these assets very risky to own.

The Relationship between Risk and Return

Significant differences are attached to owning different investments. As a general rule, investments that have exhibited a history of unusually high returns tend to produce returns that are very difficult to forecast. Over a period of many years, common stocks have provided investors with higher but less predictable returns than bonds. Stocks don't outperform bonds in every year, of course, and stocks have produced major losses for their owners in some years. There are significant differences in risk among different types of bonds. Corporate bonds generally provide higher but less predictable returns than U.S. Treasury bonds that, in turn, provide higher but less predictable returns than U.S. Treasury bills.

> **Tip** It is best not to be too greedy when selecting a bond to purchase. Bonds that promise an unusually high return nearly always do so because of investor concern that the promised payments of interest and principal may not be made on schedule.

Figure 13 ■ A Comparison of Risk and Expected Return for Bond Investments

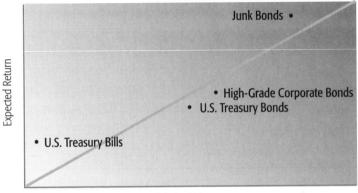

Figure 13 provides a comparison of the risk/return relationships for a variety of bonds and debt securities. The relative risk of owning an asset is measured on the horizontal axis, with less risky assets positioned toward the left side and more risky assets toward the right side. The graph indicates that corporate bonds are more risky to own than U.S. Treasury bonds, for example. The *expected* return to be earned by owning an asset is measured on the vertical axis. The higher on the graph a particular asset is positioned, the higher the rate of return the asset is expected to earn.

The upward slope of dots from the lower left to the upper right reflects the positive relationship that exists between risk and return. In general, investors dislike uncertainty and are willing to accept a lower expected return in exchange for greater certainty of the return they expect to earn from an investment. Investors purchase U.S. Treasury bills, which generally provide a very modest return, because of certainty that the modest return will be earned. Investors normally commit their money to volatile common stocks only when they expect stocks to provide substantially higher returns than the returns that are available on U.S. Treasury bills.

The Risks of Owning Bonds

Bonds subject investors to a variety of risks, some important and some not so important. Some of these risks are important to certain investors but not to other investors. A large part of the risk of being a bondholder stems from the fixed cash payments that most bonds guarantee. Additional risk arises from the possibility that the cash payments may not occur as you expect. For example, a bond may be redeemed early, or the issuer may default on the loan agreement and stop making interest payments.

On a positive note, you have the ability to exert substantial control over most of the risks you will face from bond ownership. The key to risk control is to select bonds that best meet your particular investment needs. This seems a simple concept, but many investors are tempted to reach for extra yield, a choice that often returns to haunt them. Investing only in U.S. Treasury securities eliminates the risk that you will not receive all of a bond's scheduled payments. Selecting bonds that cannot be called by their issuer avoids the risk of an early redemption. Choosing bonds with short maturities substantially reduces the risk of large variations in the market value of debt securities. Thus, you can control the risks you face as a bondholder. Unfortunately, risk reduction isn't without a cost, and you must surrender something whenever you limit the selection of bonds to own. Stick with U.S. Treasuries and you will give up the higher returns that are available on corporate bonds. Choose only bonds that are not subject to being redeemed early and you give up the higher returns that are available on bonds that are subject to call. Invest only in short-term bonds and you surrender the higher returns generally available on bonds with long maturities.

The Risk of Unexpected Inflation

Inflation is a measure of the degree to which a good or service or a package of goods and services increases in price. Inflation means you must pay more money to purchase many of the same goods or services compared to what you paid during some past period. Inflation in the United States is measured by changes in the *consumer price index* (CPI). The *producer price index* (PPI) is a separate gauge that measures prices at the wholesale level. Changes in the producer price index—inflation at the wholesale level—often foreshadow coming inflation at the retail level.

Figure 14 (p. 124) indicates that recent inflation in the United States peaked in the late 1970s and declined throughout the 1980s, 1990s, and early 2000s. Although the recent favorable inflation statistics were good news for consumers and investors, consumer prices are subject to unexpected turns and inflation is difficult to forecast over an extended period of years. It is the unpredictability of inflation that causes bondholders to be subject to unexpected losses.

How Inflation Affects Bondholders

Unexpected inflation is a major risk faced by owners of bonds with intermediate and long maturities. A bondholder is subject to greater risk from unexpected inflation the longer the maturity length of a bond that is owned. Rising prices for bread, haircuts, heating oil, and hospital stays are bad news for a bondholder who receives a stream of fixed payments and the eventual return of a specific amount of money (that is, the face

Figure 14 ■ Annual Inflation Rates, 1965–2002

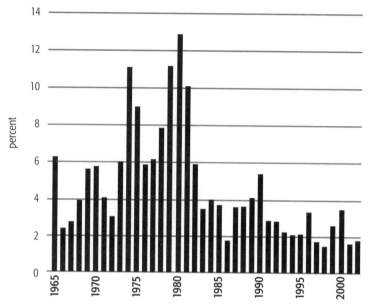

value of the bonds). The higher the rate of inflation that occurs during the period a bond is owned, the fewer goods and services each subsequent interest payment and the principal will buy. Inflation over a period of 20 or 30 years can eat away a significant portion of the purchasing power of a bond's principal payment.

Invest in bonds and you know the size of the cash payments you will receive and when the payments will be received. Unfortunately, you don't know what the cash will buy at the time it is received. Will the principal that is returned in 10 years buy 80 percent of what the same amount of money will buy today? Perhaps, 70 percent? Half? If consumer prices remain constant, that is, no inflation occurs, interest and principal will be worth just as much when you receive them as they are worth today. If inflation occurs at an annual rate of 7 percent, an interest payment in ten years will have about half the purchasing power of the same interest payment today.

The inflation-adjusted return that is earned on an investment is known as the *real return*. If you purchase a bond that promises an annual return of 7 percent during a period when you expect inflation to average 3 percent annually, you will anticipate earning an annual real return of 4 percent. The real return is positive whenever you earn a return that is higher than the rate of inflation. A positive real return means the investment provides a high enough return that you are able to increase the overall purchasing power of your investment. As an investor you should be more concerned about an investment's real return than about the nominal or stated return. A bond paying 5 percent during a time when inflation is 2 percent is a better investment than a bond paying 9 percent during a period when inflation is 7 percent. The 5-percent bond provides a real return of 3 percent while the 9-percent bond provides a real return of only 2 percent.

The returns offered by bonds are influenced by the inflation rate that is anticipated by both borrowers and lenders. A lender can be expected to seek a higher interest rate on a loan when a high rate of inflation is anticipated. At the same time, a borrower who expects to repay a loan in dollars of reduced value will be more willing to pay a higher interest rate to borrow money. The

Tip Unexpected inflation is a major risk to holders of bonds with long maturities. Substantial inflation over a period of years can devastate the purchasing power of interest payments and the principal to be returned at maturity.

> **Tip** Interest rates are strongly influenced by inflationary expectations. If investors revise upward their inflationary forecasts you can expect interest rates to also move upward. The rise in interest rates will result in a fall in bond values. Thus, bond values are inversely related not only to market rates of interest but also to inflationary expectations.

bottom line is that inflationary expectations are built into interest rates and bond yields. Expectations for higher inflation can cause higher interest rates and higher bond yields. Investors who purchase bonds are compensated for expected inflation with higher yields on their investments. High-quality bonds with a 15-year maturity might yield 6 percent at a time when inflation of 3 percent is expected, whereas the same bonds might yield 8 percent when inflation of 5 percent is expected.

If inflation is offset by higher interest rates, how can rising consumer prices be considered a risk factor of owning bonds? The answer is that only *expected* inflation is offset by higher interest rates. If the actual rate of inflation turns out to be higher than expected inflation, then all lenders, including bondholders, will be negatively affected because the real returns they earn will be smaller than they anticipated when the terms of the loans were arranged. If you expect annual inflation of approximately 3 percent during the next 15 years, you may feel comfortable purchasing a 15-year bond that yields 6 percent. If things work out as you anticipate, the bond will provide an inflation adjusted, or real return, of 3 percent. Suppose that inflation proves to be much worse than you expect and climbs to 8 percent. Now you find that consumer prices are increasing so rapidly that you are earning a real return that is negative.

Reducing the Risk from Inflation

Investors who purchase bonds with long maturities are subject to the greatest possibility of loss from unexpected inflation. One reason for the greater risk associated with long-term bonds is that inflation is more difficult to accurately forecast many years in the future. You may have a good feeling about your ability to estimate the inflation rate for the next couple of years, but what about the inflation rate 10 or 15 years from now? Forecasting inflation many years down the road is a task that stumps even the best economists. The more difficult it is for you to accurately forecast inflation, the more risk there is to owning bonds.

Another reason that long-term bonds are subject to so much risk from inflation is that unexpectedly high inflation over many years can absolutely devastate the purchasing power of a fixed sum of money. An annual average inflation rate of 7 percent over 20 years causes $100 to have a purchasing power of only about $25 in the 20th year. Suppose you purchase $10,000 principal amount of a 20-year maturity bond. If the annual inflation rate is 7 percent over the life of the bond, the $10,000 face value returned at maturity will buy only $2,500 in goods and services compared to what you could buy with the same $10,000 today. You may receive the money that is promised, but it just might not be worth much.

If long-term bonds subject you to more risk from unexpected inflation, the obvious way to avoid this risk is to invest in bonds with short maturities. The shorter the maturity of a bond, the less you need to worry about interest and principal payments being undermined by inflation. If inflation spurts upward, causing the investment community to revise upward the prevailing expectation regarding inflation, higher interest rates will result. Buy bonds with short maturities and you will have to wait only a short time before the bond is redeemed and you are able to either spend the money before prices go up further, or reinvest the money at the new, higher interest rate.

The Risk of Rising Interest Rates

The possibility of rising interest rates can be a serious concern for investors who purchase bonds with long maturities. The fixed interest payments you receive as the owner of a bond are likely to seem inadequate when market rates of interest experience a sharp increase. If you invest in a bond just prior to a major increase in interest rates, you are likely to kick yourself for not having waited a little longer before committing your funds.

The market values of outstanding bonds are negatively affected by rising interest rates. Bonds with long maturities are affected much more than bonds with short maturities, and bonds with low coupon rates are affected more than bonds with high coupon rates. A long-term, zero-coupon bond is the worst possible debt security to own during a period when market interest rates are rising. A bond that matures within a year is the best possible debt security to own when interest rates are headed upward.

Why Maturity Length Is Important

Owning a bond that has a long maturity means that you have committed money to earning the same annual income for many years. You can always sell the bond prior to maturity, of course, but at the time you purchase the bond there is no way to determine what price you will receive from a sale prior to maturity.

Suppose you invest $10,000 in a new issue of municipal bonds that has a coupon of 5 percent and a 25-year maturity. You will receive 5 percent of $10,000, or $500 in annual interest for 25 years, at which time the bond's $10,000 principal will

> **Tip** Rising interest rates are not an important risk for short-term bonds because bonds with short maturities will not decline much in response to an increase in market rates of interest. In addition, at maturity the principal can be reinvested at a higher interest rate. Rising interest rates have a much greater negative impact on the prices of bonds with long maturities.

be returned to you. If the bonds are subject to being redeemed early, your money may be returned prior to the scheduled maturity.

Five years following purchase of the bonds, long-term interest rates have increased to the point where new bonds of similar maturity (now, 20 years) and risk are being issued with 8-percent coupons. A $10,000 investment in newly issued bonds will produce annual interest income of $800 (8 percent of $10,000) compared to the $500 you are receiving now. It should be obvious that no one will be willing to pay $10,000 for your bonds should you decide to sell. If you sell the bonds now, you must accept a relatively low price compared to the price you paid when interest rates were lower. The bonds you own will lock whoever owns them into receiving only $500 annually for another 20 years. Just think, this is 20 years during which a bondholder will earn $300 per year less than the income that is being paid by newly issued bonds. Twenty years is a long time to earn a substandard income, and any investor is going to consider this penalty when they make an offer to purchase the bonds you want to sell.

Suppose you initially purchased a bond with a maturity of 10 years rather than 25 years. In other words, you decided to purchase a bond that was scheduled for redemption 15 years earlier than the 25-year bond. Although yields are generally lower for bonds with reduced maturity lengths, assume the coupon on the 10-year bond is 5-percent, the same as the 25-year bond. The only difference between the bonds is the 10-year bond returns its principal 15 years earlier than the 25-year bond. Five years down the road following the increase in interest rates, new bonds with a 5-year maturity (your bond now has 5 years remaining to maturity) yield 8 percent. If you decide to sell this bond, you should not suffer as large a loss as on the 25-year bond because a buyer will earn a substandard annual income for only another 5 years. The fewer years an investor must accept a reduced annual income, the less a bond's price is penalized. Translated, this means that a given change in interest rates will have less effect on the market value of a bond with a short maturity than on the market value of a bond with a long maturity. The shorter a bond's maturity, the less the bond will vary in price because of interest rate changes.

The other side of the coin is that bonds with long maturities increase in price more than short-term bonds when interest rates decline. If you expect interest rates to fall during the next several years, you would enjoy a larger gain by owning a bond with a long maturity than by owning a bond with a short maturity. Bonds with long maturities decline more in value when interest rates rise but increase more in market value when interest rates decline.

Figure 15 illustrates the prices at which bonds of various maturity lengths should sell in several different interest rate environments. Interest rates are displayed at the top of each column. All the values are calculated for a bond with a 7-percent coupon and a $1,000 face value. Maturity lengths for each bond are listed in the first column. When the market rate of interest is 7 percent, a bond with a 7-percent coupon will sell at a price

Figure 15 ■ Maturity Length, Interest Rates, and Bond Values
(Values for a $1,000 principal amount, 7-percent coupon bond)

Maturity Length	Market Interest Rate					
	3%	5%	7%	10%	12%	15%
1 year	$1,039	$1,019	$1,000	$973	$955	$930
3 years	1,131	1,039	1,000	925	880	817
5 years	1,123	1,087	1,000	886	820	732
10 years	1,336	1,154	1,000	816	717	598
15 years	1,478	1,208	1,000	772	659	517
25 years	1,697	1,282	1,000	728	608	483

equal to its par value regardless of the bond's maturity. Bonds must always sell at a discount when the coupon rate of interest is less than the going market rate of interest. For example, a market rate of interest of more than 7 percent means a bond with a 7-percent coupon must sell for less than its face value regardless of the bond's maturity length. The longer a bond's maturity, the greater the discount from face value at which the bond should sell. For example, a 7-percent coupon bond that matures in 15 years will sell for $659 when the market rate of interest for similar bonds is 12 percent. A bond with a 5-year maturity length should sell for $820 in a market that demands a 12-percent yield.

Why a Bond's Coupon Size Is Important

A bond that has a relatively high coupon (for example, an 8-percent coupon, as opposed to a 6-percent or 5-percent coupon) returns cash to a bondholder more rapidly because a larger proportion of the bond's total cash flow consists of interest payments. A high coupon and the more rapid return of cash causes the bond's market price to be influenced less by interest rate changes compared to a bond of the same maturity that has a low coupon. Remember, the sooner a bond's scheduled payments, the less the current value of those payments is influenced by changing interest rates. As mentioned previously in this chapter, the values of zero-coupon bonds, especially zero-coupon bond issues with long maturities, are strongly affected by interest rate changes. A zero-coupon bond's price is strongly susceptible to interest rate changes because the bondholder must wait the entire life of the bond before any cash payment is received.

Suppose you are considering an investment in a bond but are concerned that interest rates will be higher several years down the road. One solution is to buy a bond with a short maturity. This bond will mature in several years and allow you to reinvest the principal at a higher yield than is available today. At least, this will be the result if your forecast of higher interest rates proves correct. You consider this option but decide that you are unwilling to sacrifice the higher yields that are currently available on bonds with longer maturities. A second option is to ask that your broker search the secondary market for a bond that has a high coupon compared to the coupons being offered on newly issued bonds. Even though a high-coupon bond will sell at a large premium to par, price fluctuations caused by interest rate changes will be relatively small compared to bonds that have low coupons.

The reduced price fluctuations of high-coupon bonds mean that high-coupon bonds are generally less risky to own than low-coupon bonds. This comparison assumes that bonds have equal maturity lengths. At the same time that high-coupon bonds are less risky to own, these bonds have a reduced potential for gains in value. A high-coupon bond loses less market value when interest rates rise, but gains less market value when interest rates decline.

The Risk of Falling Interest Rates

Lower interest rates are a risk both for bondholders who plan to reinvest interest income and principal and for bondholders who rely upon interest income to pay for current spending. Falling interest rates are not an important issue for an investor who expects to spend both the interest and principal from a bond. However, if you purchase a bond with the intention of reinvesting all of the bond's interest payments, falling interest rates will cause you to earn a reduced return on the reinvested interest payments than if interest rates stayed constant or increased. You also incur a risk if you intend to reinvest the bond's principal, especially if the principal is scheduled for return relatively soon.

Suppose you examine the interest rates available on bonds of different maturities and discover that not much difference exists between the yields of 1-year bonds and the yields of 20-year bonds. A similar yield for bonds of all maturity lengths is called a *flat yield curve*. A flat yield curve is relatively rare but it does occur from time to time. You know that bonds with longer maturities are subject to greater price fluctuations (we discussed this earlier in this chapter), so you play it safe and choose a bond with a 1-year maturity. Interest rates begin to decline soon after you purchase the bond, and when your bond is redeemed at the end of the year, interest rates are several percentage points below the rate you earned on the redeemed bond. If you reinvest the bond's principal, your annual interest income will be substantially below interest income earned during the first year. Whether you choose to reinvest the year's interest income or use the interest to pay for consumption, you have ended up in a worsened financial position because you chose the short-term bond that you considered the low-risk alternative. If you had chosen a bond with a longer maturity you would continue to earn the higher return from that security until it is redeemed. This example illustrates that even short-term bonds of high quality can subject their owners to a certain degree of risk. Just ask the millions of people who had large investments in money market accounts and short-term certificates of deposit during the early 2000s when short-term interest rates experienced a major and rapid decline.

The method for reducing the risk of falling interest rates is obvious: Invest in bonds that have low coupons and long maturities. A long-term, zero-coupon bond is the ultimate protection against falling interest rates because zero-coupon bonds pay no interest income that must be reinvested and the principal will not be returned for many years. Although a long-term, zero-coupon bond provides protection against falling interest rates, the bond's market value will suffer a major decline in the event market rates of interest increase. Indeed, there is no perfect investment, even in the world of high-quality bonds.

The Risk of Not Being Paid

Most bonds subject investors to at least some risk that payments will not be made as promised. The risk of nonpayment is especially important for investors who hold bonds issued by financially ailing organizations. In a worst-case scenario, a borrower suffers substantial losses over several years before throwing in the towel and declaring bankruptcy. All interest and principal payments cease at bankruptcy and after several years of legal proceedings few assets remain for distribution to the firm's creditors. If you are a bondholder of this company, you may lose nearly all of your investment. More than a few investors have purchased municipal and corporate bonds only to watch their investment virtually disappear from a borrower's default.

Bondholders have a legal claim to interest and principal, but the financial condition of a borrower can sometimes deteriorate so quickly that the bondholders are unable to recover much of the debt they are owed simply because the firm has nothing valuable remaining. The likelihood of interest and principal not being paid is much greater if you own debentures or subordinated debentures—debt securities that do not have a claim to specific assets or groups of assets.

Causes of Nonpayment

Companies are subject to uncertainties caused by the nature of the industry in which they operate. For example, an industry may be unusually competitive, which often results in low profits or losses for many of the firms. Another industry may be built around an emerging technology and include companies that are spending large sums of money without any guarantee that profits will result. Other companies enter periods of poor operating conditions because of poor management decisions. Managers may build too many plants, produce a product that not enough people want to buy, hire too many employees, or choose the wrong technology. Buying bonds issued by companies with an uncertain future creates risk that the issuers will be unable to meet all of their scheduled debt payments in a timely manner.

Concern about changing economic activity and fluctuating revenues also applies to owners of municipal bonds. Cities, school districts, hospitals, and counties have been known to stop paying interest on their debts. A city may pledge tax revenues as a guarantee to bondholders, but if most of the town's citizens

> **Tip** Individual investors should generally stay away from bonds that are unrated by one of the major rating companies. Corporations and municipalities planning to issue bonds can choose to forgo a rating for a number of valid reasons; however, no rating means that it is difficult for an individual to judge the credit risk associated with a particular bond issue.

move elsewhere, little income and few assets of any value may remain to tax. An inability to service debt is a special concern when a town or region relies heavily on a single business or a single industry to provide most of the jobs and tax revenues.

Payment of interest and principal may stop because of financial reasons. Businesses and governments sometimes borrow so much money that they have difficulty servicing their debts even during periods of favorable economic conditions. Even a company with stable revenues and expenses can handle only so much debt. Likewise, a city with a strong tax base can borrow such a large amount of money that it has difficulty making the required interest and principal payments. The more money a particular company or municipality borrows, the more likely the borrower will encounter financial difficulty down the road.

Bond Ratings

Most individuals who are interested in purchasing bonds do not have the time, interest, or expertise to analyze the financial strength of a borrower or the credit quality of a bond issue. Even many institutional investors are unable to examine the credit quality of all the bond issues they consider buying for their portfolios. Fortunately, several companies are in the business of evaluating the quality of debt issues.

> **Tip** Ratings of corporate bonds sometimes change over their lifetime. A bond that is rated AA at the time it is issued may later be downgraded to A or even lower. Likewise, a bond's rating is sometimes raised in the event the issuer becomes financially stronger. A decline in a bond's rating is likely to cause a decline in the bond's market value.

Chapter 1 discussed the bond rating companies that employ financial analysts who examine and grade fixed-income securities. These firms charge issuers a fee to grade their bonds. The rating awarded to a bond issue has a major impact on the interest rate the issuer will have to pay in order to sell the issue to investors. Investors evaluating bonds to acquire consider ratings to be such an important factor that many issues would be difficult or impossible to distribute without an independent rating.

The rating companies each have somewhat different but similar classifications for bonds. Bonds are grouped into ten to twelve quality categories. The three major rating companies—Moody's, Standard & Poor's, and Fitch—have AAA as their most credit-worthy category in which only the highest-quality bonds are included. Many financial advisers suggest that individual investors restrict their purchases to bonds that qualify for the top two or three categories. Bonds rated lower than BBB (S&P and Fitch) or Baa (Moody's) are generally considered fairly risky and qualify as *junk bonds*. Figure 16 (p. 138) illustrates the rating categories with a short explanation of each category.

The Risk of Difficulty in Selling a Bond

Bonds are not always easy to resell in the event you decide to liquidate your investment prior to the scheduled maturity. If you

Figure 16 ■ Bond Credit Ratings

S&P	Moody's	Fitch	
AAA	Aaa	AAA	High-grade with extremely strong capacity to pay principal and interest
AA	Aa	AA	High-grade by all standards but with slightly lower margins of protection than AAA
A	A	A	Medium-grade with favorable investment attributes but some susceptibility to adverse economic conditions
BBB	Baa	BBB	Medium-grade with adequate capacity to pay interest and principal but possibly lacking certain protection against adverse economic conditions
BB	Ba	BB	Speculative with moderate protection of principal and interest in an unstable economy
B	B	B	Speculative and lacking desirable characteristics of investment bonds. Small assurance principal and interest will be paid on schedule
CCC	Caa	CCC	In default or in danger of default
CC	Ca	CC	Highly speculative and in default or with some other market shortcomings
C	C	C	Extremely poor investment quality. Paying no interest
D		D	In default with interest or principal in arrears

are absolutely certain to hold a bond until maturity, the bond's lack of liquidity isn't an important consideration. On the other hand, if there is some possibility you will want to sell a bond

THE RISKS OF INVESTING IN BONDS

before it is scheduled for redemption by the issuer, you may be unpleasantly surprised by the price you receive.

Many bond issues—both corporate and municipal—rarely trade in the secondary market. An inactive bond is likely to suffer from a relatively large difference between the price at which it can be bought and the price at which it can be sold. The large spread means you are likely to receive what you may consider an inadequate price in the event you attempt to sell a bond that is infrequently traded. Of course, you can avoid the risk of owning an inactive bond by restricting purchases to bonds with an active secondary market.

You may encounter another problem related to liquidity if you purchase relatively few bonds. Bonds tend to trade in large quantities. That is, a standard unit of trading bonds is $25,000, $50,000, or, in some cases, $250,000. Selling bonds in small lots means you are likely to be penalized with regard to the price you receive. Dealers are likely to show little interest in acquiring securities they will have difficulty reselling. Dealers often reduce the price at which they will sell a small number of bonds in order to clear the securities from their portfolios. The willingness to lower the price at which dealers will sell a small lot of bonds means these same dealers are likely to reduce the price they will pay to buy a small lot of bonds. Keep in mind that the bond market is primarily designed for major players such as insurance companies, pension funds, mutual funds, and commercial banks. These institutions engage in enormous trades amounting to many millions of dollars. Dealers who buy bonds for resale are not likely to be enthusiastic about acquiring a small number of bonds from you when they know they are likely to have difficulty reselling the bonds at a competitive yield.

Several avenues are available to compensate for the fact that bonds may be difficult to sell. You should generally purchase bonds with maturities that are in line with your financial goals so that you will be able to hold the bonds until their scheduled redemption. Individual investors are nearly always better off when they are able to hold bonds issues until maturity. In the event you feel that long-term bonds offer too good a yield to turn down, consider limiting your selections to bonds that are part of large issues from well-known issuers. Small bond issues from little-known issuers are almost certain to suffer from modest trading activity in the secondary market. A knowledge-able broker should be able to steer you to bonds that are likely to have a relatively active secondary market. Another method for overcoming the liquidity problem of individual bond issues is to buy shares of mutual funds or closed-end investment companies that invest in bonds. Investment company shares are easily sold, and expenses can be nominal. Be certain to investigate a fund's fees before investing.

Bonds as One Part of a Diversified Portfolio

It is very risky and nearly always a mistake to commit all your funds to a single type of investment, and bonds are no exception. No matter how carefully you consider the quality and maturities of bonds, these financial assets, by themselves, are not likely to produce either the returns or the reduction in risk you can obtain with a diversified portfolio that includes bonds, stocks, and tangible assets. This is especially true over a period of many years when you can expect the returns from a portfolio of equities and tangible assets to exceed the returns from either long-term or short-term bonds.

Combining stocks and tangible assets with bonds allows you to reduce some of the risks that strongly impact bond investments, especially unexpected inflation that reduces the purchasing power of fixed payments. Even though common stocks by themselves are considered more risky to own than bonds, combining common stocks with an existing portfolio of bonds can reduce the risk of your overall portfolio while simultaneously increasing the portfolio's expected return. The reduced risk of a diversified portfolio stems from the fact that returns from different types of investments do not always move together. That is, returns from common stocks, bonds, and tangible assets do not increase and decline together. While news of a very strong economy might be good for owners of stocks and tangible assets, it is not particularly favorable for bondholders who are likely to be concerned about upward pressure on consumer prices and interest rates. Increases in consumer prices cause interest and principal to have less purchasing power, while higher interest rates cause a decline in the market value of a bond.

The reduced risk of a diversified portfolio does not mean you can overlook the specific risks of bonds that were discussed earlier in this chapter. It is still important to select bonds with maturity lengths that match your investment goals. It is also important to choose bond investments with a level of credit risk that matches your own risk profile. In other words, don't concentrate your investment in long-term bonds when you are likely to require substantial amounts of cash on short notice. Likewise, don't choose bonds with low credit ratings when you cannot afford the possibility of reduced income or loss of principal.

> **Tip** Financial advisers generally suggest that individual investors limit their purchases to bond issues rated A or higher. A higher rating means a reduced yield but greater certainty that interest and principal will be paid as promised.

8 Sources of Information about Bonds

Developing a successful program for investing in bonds requires that you be able to locate relevant information about bond issuers, individual bond issues, and investment companies that invest in bonds. In general, information about bonds is in less demand and is less readily available than information about stocks. A limited number of bond price quotations are available in several financial publications and in the business section of some daily newspapers. Price quotations for mutual funds and investment companies are in these same publications. Details about individual bond issues are on Internet sites and in several publications available in many libraries.

To be an informed investor you must be able to locate information about investments in which you have an interest. In the case of bonds, you should know how to obtain price quotations and understand what these quotations indicate. You should also know where to obtain information about organizations that issue bonds along with more general information about a particular industry and the overall economy. For example, it is important to check current market interest rates and inflation rates in order to judge whether a bond's yield is adequate. This chapter will point you toward some of the more readily available sources of useful information about bond investments.

Bond Price Quotations

Bond price quotations are generally more difficult to locate than quotations for stocks and mutual funds. As discussed in Chapter 5, most corporate bonds, municipal bonds, U.S. Treasury bonds, and federal agency bonds are traded over-the-counter rather than on an organized exchange. Limited corporate bond price quotations are published daily in *The Wall Street Journal* and weekly in *Barron's*. Some large daily newspapers carry a partial listing of corporate bonds that are traded on organized exchanges. Price quotations for U.S. Treasury bills, notes, and bonds and for federal agency bonds are published in *The Wall Street Journal* and *Barron's* and in some large daily newspapers. Quotes for U.S. Treasury securities are generally more easily located than are quotes for corporate bonds.

Price quotations for municipal bonds and for corporate bonds that trade in the over-the-counter market are more difficult to obtain. You must usually contact a brokerage company in order to acquire current price quotations for OTC bonds. A brokerage firm with a large bond operation should be able to supply a bond price quotation relatively quickly unless the bond is particularly obscure. Some brokerage firms include on their website a posting of bonds available for sale.

Bond prices are nearly always quoted as a percentage of par value. For example, a municipal or corporate bond price quota-

Tip Only a small number of corporate and municipal bond price quotations are published in major newspapers including *The Wall Street Journal*. Current quotes for corporate and municipal bonds can be obtained from brokerage firms that have access to bond desks and from several Internet sites.

tion of 82 1/2 indicates a selling price of 82.5 percent of par value, or $825 per $1,000 face value. A price of 103 means a corporate bond is trading at a price of 103 percent of par value, or $1,030. A price of 140 indicates a corporate bond traded at a price of $1,400. Corporate and municipal bonds are traded in eighths of a point, and Treasury notes and bonds are traded in thirty-seconds of a point. A point is equal to 1 percent of a bond's face value, or $10 in the case of corporate bonds. Thus, a corporate bond that declines in price by 5/8 of a point has fallen in market value by 5/8 of $10, or $6.25. A bond that increases in price by 2 1/4 points has gained $22.50 in market value.

Corporate Bond Quotations

Corporate bonds are denominated in multiples of $1,000, so a corporate bond quotation of 87 indicates that the bond is trading at a price of $870. A newspaper quotation for a corporate bond traded on the New York or American exchanges may appear as:

Bond	Cur Yld	Vol	Close	Net Ch
AT&T 6 1/2 29	7.4	150	87.38	-0.25

The listing indicates that the bond issued by AT&T has a 6 1/2-percent coupon and a scheduled maturity in the year 2029. Several publications and websites will provide information on the day and month of the interest payments and the principal repayment. Annual interest paid by the bond is 6 1/2 percent of the $1,000 face value, or $65 per year per bond. During the trading session, 150 bonds were traded and the last transaction occurred at a price of $873.80, $2.50 less than the closing price for the last previous session in which the bond traded. The current yield, calculated as annual interest ($65) divided by the closing price ($873.80), is 7.4 percent. If you

> **Tip** Information about current bond trades and yields is available on the Internet at *www.investinginbonds.com*. The site provides pricing information for recent trades of corporate, municipal, and U.S. Treasury bonds. The data can be used to compare with the bond yields offered to you by a broker. This excellent website also includes educational material about bonds.

purchased the bond at the closing price of $873.80, you would earn a yield to maturity of more than 7.4 percent because the bond will gain $126.20 in market value by the maturity date when you will receive the face value of $1,000. The yield to maturity is not indicated in the listing but can be calculated or supplied by a broker.

Municipal bond price quotations are identical to corporate price quotations. That is, municipal bonds are quoted in eighths of a point, and current yield and yield to maturity are calculated in the same manner as for corporate bonds. Municipal bonds are traded in $5,000 denominations, so that an offering quotation of 90 equates to a bond price of 90 percent of $5,000, or $4,500. Most readily available publications do not include municipal bond quotations, although several publications including *The Wall Street Journal* and *Barron's* have very limited price listings and include general information about the municipal bond market. Pricing for recent municipal and corporate bond trades is available online without charge at *www.investingin bonds.com*.

Treasury and Federal Agency Security Quotations

Quotations for Treasury notes and bonds and for federal agency securities frequently appear as:

Rate	Maturity Mo/Yr	Bid	Asked	Chg	Ask Yld
5.000	Feb 11n	107:22	107:23	6	3.88

The listing is for a Treasury note (denoted by n beside the maturity date) with a 5-percent coupon and a February 2011 maturity date. Pricing information for Treasury notes and bonds often includes closing bid and asked prices rather than a closing price for the last trade. The bond listed here was being offered for sale (the asked price) at 107 23/32, or $1,077.19, and dealers were offering to buy the bond at a price of 107 22/32, or $1,076.87. Treasury security price quotations generally apply to very large transactions typically undertaken only by institutional investors. Individual investors incur a slightly lower bid price and a slightly higher asked price than indicated by the quotations. The change of 6 indicates the price at the close of the trading session was 6/32 lower than the price at the close of the previous session. The bond provided a yield to maturity of 3.88 percent based on the asked price. The asked price is used because it is the price that is being offered to buyers of the security. The note's current yield is not indicated but is easily calculated as $50/$1,077.19, or 4.64 percent.

Quotations for Treasury bills are published in a somewhat different fashion from quotations for Treasury notes and bonds. Bid and asked quotes for Treasury bills are in hundredths, quoted as a percentage discount from face value. For example, a bid quotation of 2.80 means the dealer is offering to buy Treasury bills of a particular maturity at a discount of 2.8 percent from face value. Thus, $10,000 face value of these particular bills could be sold for $9,720. Treasury bill quotations do not include a coupon rate because Treasury bills sell at a discount rather than pay semiannual interest. Like quotations for Treasury bonds and notes, published Treasury bill bid and ask quotations generally apply to very large transactions.

Mutual Fund Quotations

Most large daily newspapers publish mutual fund price quotations, although the listings are sometimes selective and frequently abbreviated. Published quotations generally consist of the net asset value (NAV) and the change in the closing NAV compared to the closing NAV for the previous trading session. Mutual fund shares are quoted in dollars and cents per share and typically appear as:

	NAV	NAV Chg
GrnAcreLT	9.78	−.26

The listing indicates that shares of the Green Acres Long-Term Bond Fund have a net asset value of $9.78 per share. During the trading session the shares declined by 26¢ compared to the closing net asset value during the previous session. The price decline means you would have lost $130 if you owned 500 shares of the fund. Listings sometimes indicate whether a fund levies a sales charge or 12b–1 fee. Some listings also provide the percentage return that the fund has provided since the beginning of the year.

> **Tip** Many bond issues are of relatively small size and are rarely traded in the secondary market, making it difficult to obtain accurate pricing information. Purchase corporate or municipal bonds and you are likely to be disappointed if you expect to look in the morning paper and see how your investment performed during the previous day's trading.

Sources of Bond Information

The investment decision regarding whether to purchase a particular bond should be made on the basis of more than the bond's yield. The scheduled maturity, coupon rate, issuer, sinking fund, collateral, credit rating, call feature, and other specifics that are peculiar to a bond issue influence a bond's value and its appropriateness as an investment. These features should be considerations when you are selecting a bond to purchase. For example, you may want to choose a bond with a maturity that is different from the maturities of bonds that you already own. Likewise, you may want to purchase bonds from an issuer that is different from the issuers of any of the bonds you currently own. A call provision, if any, is very important in selecting a bond to purchase. Your broker should be able to provide this information when he or she calls to inform you about bonds the firm has available for sale. Seeking information from a broker is fine so long as you are seriously considering an investment. Suppose you are in an early investigative stage and want to locate information about a dozen or more bond issues that you believe might be appropriate for your portfolio. Where should you turn when you see the disturbed look on your broker's face? The Internet offers a trove of information about bonds. Print materials are available for investors without Internet access.

Information about the Credit Markets

First things first. It is wise to become acquainted with the credit markets before you spend a lot of time investigating particular bond issuers and poring through the details of specific bond issues. What is occurring with respect to interest rates and what is the general forecast for short-term and long-term interest rate movements during the next year? What are municipal bonds yielding relative to Treasuries and corporate bonds with similar maturities? Are large volumes of new bond issues expected to come to market in the next few weeks or the next few months? Answers to these and other questions should influence your decision about whether to invest in bonds and, if so, when and what types of bonds to choose.

One readily available source of current bond market information is *The Wall Street Journal*'s daily "Credit Markets" column that provides an overview of the debt markets along with an assessment of the previous day's activity in corporate, government, and municipal bonds. The column frequently reviews new debt issues, especially issues of substantial size or from well-known borrowers. It sometimes includes insights from bond market professionals on various topics ranging from expectations about interest rate movements to actions taken by or expected by the Federal Reserve. For example, is the Fed expected to announce that it will pursue reduced short-term interest rates during its next meeting? This is an excellent source of information for keeping abreast of credit market activities. Each issue of *The Wall Street Journal* includes a listing of the previous day's new bond issues along with yields of selected corporate, municipal, and government bonds. *Barron's*, a weekly Dow Jones publication carried by nearly all libraries, includes "Economic Beat," a column devoted to economic analysis, and "Current Yield," a column about the credit markets and fixed-income investing. *Standard & Poor's Credit Week* provides information about the state of the credit markets and upcoming and recent corporate and municipal bond issues. Either *Credit Week* or a similar publication, *Mergent Bond Record,* is generally available in large libraries.

Information about Issuers

Several readily available sources provide information about particular corporations. Publications such as the *Value Line Investment Survey, Standard & Poor's Stock Reports, Mergent Handbook of Common Stocks,* and *Mergent Handbook of NASDAQ Stocks* are in most public libraries and virtually all college libraries. Each publication provides current and historical data for revenues, earnings, interest expense, assets, and debt for hundreds of companies. Years of historical data allow you to examine trends in each of these important financial statistics. The three publications include short discussions of recent developments and the outlook for each company. Although the publications are primarily intended for investors who are interested in buying common stocks, the information is also valuable for investors who are in the market to buy debt securities.

Information about issuers of municipal bonds is sometimes difficult to locate. One of the best sources for information about municipalities is *Mergent Municipal and Government Manual and News Reports,* a publication that is in many college and large public libraries. The *Manual* contains information on states, state agencies, and thousands of municipalities.

Tip U.S. Treasury bonds are actively traded and pricing is readily available in financial publications including *The Wall Street Journal* and on brokerage firm websites. Treasury securities are generally much easier to buy and sell than either corporate or municipal bonds.

Information about Specific Bond Issues

Suppose you recently heard about a particular bond issue and want to learn details about the bonds. Perhaps you want to determine if the bonds can be called and, if so, beginning when and at what price. A good and readily available source of bond details is *Mergent Bond Record*, a monthly publication carried by most college and large public libraries. This publication includes information about interest payment dates, maturity dates (day, month, and year), bond rating, sinking fund provision, call price and dates, yield, price range, and the issue price and date. A section reserved for convertible bonds includes data for interest and maturity dates, conversion price (to determine the number of shares into which a bond can be converted), yield call price, and quality rating. *Mergent Bond Record* also includes an extensive listing of municipal bond ratings. *Standard & Poor's Bond Guide* is a monthly publication that includes much of the same information contained in Mergent's Bond Record. The *Bond Guide* is available in most libraries.

Information on the Internet

The Internet serves as a handy source for information on all types of investment interests including credit market conditions and bonds. A computer and Internet connection will allow you to locate basic information about bond investments, current yields that are available on a wide variety of fixed-income securities, recent bond trades, Federal Reserve actions, and nearly anything else you might want to know. The difficulty is in identifying the best sites to provide the information you are seeking. Most online brokerage firms offer yield and credit market information, although the quantity and quality of the information is sometimes skimpy because the majority of space is devoted to equity investments. Several general interest financial sites offer

Figure 17 ■ Recommended Internet Sites for Bond Investors

General Information about the Economy and Credit Markets

http://www.smartmoney.com—General business news and personal financial advice. A special section on the economy and bonds includes current data on yields, basic information to help understand economic indicators, and background information on how to choose fixed-income investments.

http://www.cbs.marketwatch.com—Current market information slanted toward stock investors. Includes economic news and an informative section on personal finance topics.

http://money.cnn.com—General business news and personal financial advice. A special section, markets and stocks, is devoted to interest rates and information of interest to bond investors.

Information Specific to Bond Investing

http://www.bondtalk.com—Lots of information for bond investors including market analysis, news about the Federal Reserve, economic analysis, and yields. This site also includes educational material about bonds and a glossary of terminology relevant to bond investors.

http://www.bondsonline.com—Commentary and articles of interest to bond investors. Educational material includes a glossary and considerations in choosing bonds that are compatible with your investment goals. This site provides an extensive listing of bonds available for purchase.

http://www.investinginbonds.com—An excellent source of information from the Bond Market Association that includes an overview of the credit markets, basic information about all types of fixed-income investments, and links to related sites. This site includes a detailed listing of the prior day's bond transactions, useful information for determining the yields that are currently available. The site is particularly useful for investors interested in buying or selling municipal bonds.

http://www.convertbond.com—News and analysis of the convertible bond market including particulars, price, and yield information for approximately 750 convertible securities. Access to this excellent site for investors interested in convertible securities requires a fee although a two-week free trial is offered.

current information relevant to bond investors. Information of interest to bond investors is typically concentrated in a special section. Several Internet sites that specialize in information about bond investments can be excellent sources of information for news, commentary, yields, and tutorials on fixed-income investing. Figure 17 includes a summary of the information that is available on several excellent Internet sites.

Glossary

above par Designation for the market value of a bond that is priced above its face value.

accrued interest Interest that has been earned but not yet paid. Bonds accrue interest from one interest payment date to the next interest payment date.

ask The price at which a bond is being offered for sale.

baby bond A bond with a principal amount of less than $1,000.

basis point One-hundredth of one percent. Basis points are used to measure yield differences among bonds.

bearer bond A bond for which ownership is not recorded by the issuer and the owner's name is not inscribed on the certificate. Bearer bonds are no longer issued in the United States.

below par Designation for the market value of a bond that is priced at less than face value.

bid The price being offered for the purchase of a bond.

bond fund An investment company that holds a portfolio that is concentrated in bonds.

bond rating An independent judgment of the likelihood that the terms of a bond will be met by the bond's issuer.

bond swap Selling one bond and simultaneously buying another bond in order to benefit from different yields, different maturities, and so forth.

book-entry security A security for which no negotiable certificate is sent to the owner.

calendar A listing of upcoming bond issues.

call Redemption of a bond prior to the scheduled maturity.

call premium The premium above face value that a borrower must pay a bondholder to redeem a bond prior to maturity.

call protection The period during which a bond's issuer cannot force a bondholder to sell bonds back to the issuer.

capital gain The amount by which the current value of an asset exceeds the price paid for the asset.

capital loss The amount by which the current value of an asset is exceeded by the price paid for the asset.

certificate Physical evidence of bond ownership.

closed-end investment company An investment company that issues a limited number of ownership shares that are traded in the secondary market.

conversion price The price at which common stock will be exchanged for a convertible bond. The conversion price divided into the bond's face value indicates the number of shares that will be received in exchange for the bond.

corporate bond A bond issued by a private business.

coupon The annual interest rate paid on a bond stated as a percentage of the bond's face value.

current yield The percentage return from a bond as calculated by comparing annual interest income and the bond's current market price. Current yield does not take into account potential changes in a bond's market value.

dealer A market maker that buys securities for and sells securities from his or her portfolio.

debenture An unsecured bond.

denomination A bond's face value.

discount bond A bond that sells below its face value.

downgrade To reduce a bond's credit rating.

equivalent taxable yield The taxable return that must be earned to produce a yield that is the same as a tax-exempt yield.

face value See *par value.*

flat Description for a bond that trades without accrued interest. Bonds that are traded flat generally indicate the issuer is in serious financial difficulty.

general creditor A lender whose loan is unsecured.

general obligation bond (GO) A municipal bond that is guaranteed by the full resources and taxing power of the issuer. See also *revenue bond.*

Ginnie Mae pass-through A security issued by Ginnie Mae that is backed by VA and FHA mortgages. Interest and principal are passed through to owners of the securities.

high-yield bond See *junk bond.*

indenture The legal agreement between a bond issuer and bond-holders. The indenture agreement specifies interest payment dates, the maturity date, collateral (if any), the trustee, and so forth.

interest rate risk The degree to which a security is affected by changes in market rates of interest.

investment company A business that pools investors' money in a professionally managed investment portfolio.

investment-grade Description for a bond that is considered sufficiently creditworthy that it can be included in regulated institutional portfolios.

junk bond A debt security of low credit quality. Also called *high-yield bond.*

liquidity The ease with which bonds can be bought and sold.

listed bond A debt security that trades on a securities exchange.

load fund A mutual fund that charges a sales fee.

long-term Description for a bond with a long maturity length.

management fee The annual charge assessed by managers of an investment company.

maturity The date on which a bond is scheduled for redemption.

mortgage bond A bond secured by a lien on real assets.

municipal bond A debt security issued by a state, city, or other political entity.

mutual fund An investment company with an undefined number of outstanding shares that continuously redeems outstanding shares at net asset value.

National Association of Securities Dealers (NASD) An association of brokers and dealers that engage in securities transactions in the over-the-counter market.

net asset value (NAV) The value of a mutual fund's shares as calculated by dividing the number of outstanding shares into the market value of the fund's portfolio. NAV is used as the basis for determining the price at which mutual fund shares are issued and redeemed.

no-load fund A mutual fund that does not levy a sales fee on shares that are sold.

noncallable bond A bond that cannot be redeemed prior to its scheduled maturity.

not rated (NR) Designating a bond that has not been rated by one of the professional credit rating agencies.

original-issue discount (OID) The amount below face value at which a new bond is issued to investors.

over-the-counter market (OTC) A network of securities dealers connected by telephones and computers. Dealers in the OTC market act as market makers in selected securities.

par value The stated value of a bond, representing the amount the bond's holder will receive on the maturity date. Also called *face value.*

premium bond A bond that sells at a price higher than its par value.

primary market 1) The market in which securities are issued to investors. 2) The main market in which a security is traded.

principal The face amount of a bond.

private placement The sale of a bond issue to a single buyer or a small group of buyers.

public offering The sale of securities to the public.

purchasing power risk The possibility that payments from an investment will lose purchasing power because of unexpected inflation. Long-term bonds subject investors to substantial purchasing power risk.

put To force an issuer to redeem a bond prior to maturity.

rating See *bond rating.*

real interest rate The stated interest rate adjusted downward for inflation.

redemption Retirement of a debt security.

reinvestment rate The annual rate of return at which an investment's cash flows can be reinvested.

revenue bond A municipal bond for which repayment of principal and interest depends upon money that is generated by the particular project the bonds are used to finance. Revenue bonds tend to have a weaker promise and more credit risk than general obligation bonds.

risk The uncertainty of the return an investment will earn.

scale The schedule of yields at different maturity lengths on a new bond issue.

secondary market The market in which outstanding securities are traded among investors and dealers.

senior debt A class of debt that has priority over one or more other debt issues of the same borrower.

serial bonds Bonds of a single issue that are scheduled to mature periodically. Many municipal bond issues are comprised of serial bonds.

settlement date The date on which cash or securities must be delivered to complete a securities transaction.

short-term Describing a bond that has a short maturity length.

sinking fund A fund for the orderly retirement of debt.

spread The difference between a bond's bid and ask price.

subordinated debenture Unsecured debt with a weak claim to payment.

syndicate A group of investment banking firms engaged in distributing an issue of securities.

term bonds An issue of bonds that all mature on the same date.

unit investment trust (UIT) An unmanaged portfolio of bonds selected by a sponsor that sells units of the trust to the public.

U.S. savings bond A nonmarketable bond issued and guaranteed by the U.S. Treasury. Series EE savings bonds are issued at a discount and earn variable returns pegged to yields on U.S. Treasury securities. Series I savings bonds are issued at face value and earn a variable return adjusted for inflation.

U.S. Treasury bill A short-term debt security of the U.S. Treasury that is issued at a discount from face value.

U.S. Treasury bond A long-term debt security issued and guaranteed by the U.S. Treasury.

U.S. Treasury note An intermediate-term debt security of the U.S. Treasury.

yield curve The relationship between yields and maturity lengths for a particular type of debt security.

yield to call The annual return earned on a bond based on the assumption the bond will be redeemed prior to maturity.

yield to maturity The annual return earned on a bond based on the assumption the bond will be held until the scheduled maturity date.

zero-coupon bond A long-term debt security that is issued at a large discount from face value and that does not make periodic interest payments.

Index

About the Author

David L. Scott has taught finance and investing at the college and university level for over thirty years. During this period he has conducted workshops, written numerous articles, and authored nearly two dozen books on business finance, personal finance, and investing. He has been a guest on numerous radio shows and appeared on NBC's *Today* and on CNBC. Dr. Scott was born in Rushville, Indiana, and received degrees from Purdue University and Florida State University before earning a PhD in economics from the University of Arkansas.